# MASTERING PYTHON FOR ARTIFICIAL INTELLIGENCE

# MASTERING PYTHON FOR ARTIFICIAL INTELLIGENCE

*Learn the Essential Coding Skills to Build Advanced AI Applications*

By

**David Ward**

# Contents

# INTRODUCTION

Python, a programming language renowned even beyond the realm of technology, has gained substantial recognition. Yet, what sets Python apart from other prominent coding languages such as Java and C++? Python stands as a widely employed, high-level programming language with a general-purpose nature. Conceived by Guido van Rossum in 1991 and fostered by the Python Software Foundation, it was primarily fashioned to prioritize code comprehensibility, enabling programmers to express concepts concisely.

In the late 1980s, the stage was set for history in the making. Python's inception was underway, with Guido Van Rossum initiating its development in December of 1989 at Centrum Wiskunde & Informatica (CWI) in the Netherlands. Initially, it emerged as a passion project, as Guido sought an engaging endeavour to occupy himself during the festive season. Python's forerunner was the ABC Programming Language, which featured interaction with the Amoeba Operating System and boasted exceptional handling capabilities.

Having contributed to the creation of ABC earlier in his career, Guido identified certain shortcomings while recognizing its commendable attributes. Ingeniously, he adopted the syntax and incorporated favorable elements from ABC. Though not without its fair share of grievances, Guido dedicatedly resolved these issues, birthing a refined scripting language that overcame all its flaws. The appellation "Python" drew inspiration from the BBC TV Show, "Monty Python's Flying Circus," as Guido held profound admiration for the series. He sought a concise, distinctive, and slightly enigmatic name for his creation, ultimately settling on "Python." Guido served as the "Benevolent dictator for life" (BDFL) until relinquishing leadership on July 12, 2018, and presently, he is employed at Dropbox, having previously worked at Google.

The language was officially unleashed in 1991, astonishingly requiring far fewer lines of code compared to Java, C++, and C to articulate concepts. Python's design philosophy proved commendable, striving to enhance code legibility and foster heightened developer productivity. Upon its release, Python showcased an impressive array of features, encompassing class inheritance, diverse core data types, exception handling, and functions, fulfilling the needs of developers proficiently.

*The chronology and examples of various Python versions are provided below:*

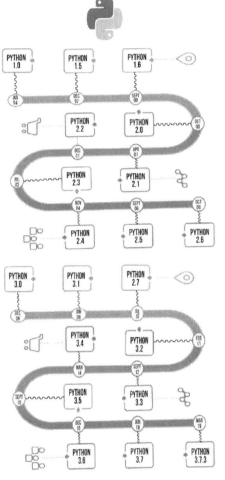

Python 3.10.4 is the latest stable version.

Python 2.x and 3.x are the most often used versions. There is a lot of competition between the two, and they both appear to have a diverse audience.

This language is used for a variety of applications, including development, scripting, generating, and software testing. Python has been adopted by prominent technological companies such as Dropbox, Google, Quora, Mozilla, Hewlett-Packard, Qualcomm, IBM, and Cisco due to it's elegance and simplicity.

Python has made remarkable strides to claim its position as the most widely adopted programming language globally. Having recently celebrated its 30th anniversary, Python continues to captivate the programming community. An exciting development took place at PyCon22, the esteemed Python conference, where the Anaconda Foundation unveiled a groundbreaking feature known as "pyscript." This innovation enables Python to be written and executed directly within web browsers, a capability previously absent. With this significant advancement, Python expands its horizons and aligns itself with the likes of JavaScript, bridging the gap between web-based programming and

Python's versatile ecosystem. Before we move on let me tell you a few things about myself.

I am David Ward, a writer, computer enthusiast, and technology expert, born in 1991 in the beautiful state of California.

With relentless determination, I pursued my dreams and graduated from the University of California at the tender age of 24, armed with a degree in computer engineering.

For over five years, I have been offering my expertise as a computer consultant to individuals and companies alike. However, in the past two years, my focus has shifted exclusively towards crafting and marketing mobile applications for startups.

It dawned on me that numerous people find it challenging to navigate through software, understand the intricacies of their workplace programs, or even unlock the full potential of their smartphones. This realization inspired me to organize courses specifically designed to help individuals, including the elderly, appreciate the immense utility of technology.

Driven by my desire to make technology accessible to everyone, I made the decision to write comprehensive, step-by-step guides.

The current version of my guide is centered around Python—a powerful programming language with a myriad of applications. Python is known for its simplicity and versatility, making it an ideal choice for beginners and seasoned programmers alike. In the following sections, we will explore the remarkable features of Python, unlocking its potential and shedding light on the numerous possibilities it holds.

Join me on this journey as we delve into the world of Python, uncovering its secrets and unraveling the magic behind its syntax. Together, we will master this remarkable language, empowering ourselves to create innovative solutions and shape the technological landscape of tomorrow.

## PYTHON'S NOTABLE FEATURES

**Python has several features, which are mentioned below:**
*

**Easy to Learn and Use**
In comparison to other programming languages, Python is simple to learn and use. It is a high-level programming language that is user-friendly for developers.

Interpreted Language
Python is an interpreted language since it does not require compilation. This simplifies debugging and makes it appropriate for novices.

### Cross-platform Language

Python may operate on a variety of platforms, including Windows, Linux, Unix, and Macintosh. As a result, we may state that Python is a portable language.

### Free and Open Source

The Python interpreter is free to install, use, and share since it is produced under an open-source license.

### Object-Oriented Language

Python allows object oriented programming, and the ideas of classes and objects emerge.

### GUI Programming Support

Python may be used to create graphical user interfaces.

### Integrated

It is simple to integrate with languages such as C, C++, and JAVA.

## PYTHON IDE INSTALLATION

**The following is a step-by-step guide for downloading and installing Python on Windows:**

**Step 1**: To download and install Python, go to the Python official website, https://www.python.org/downloads/, and select your version. Python version 3.6.3 was chosen.

**Step 2**: Run the.exe file to install Python after the download is complete. Now, select Install Now.

**Step 3**: Python is now being installed.

**Step 4:** When it is finished, you will receive a screen stating that the Setup was successful. Now press the "Close" button.

Windows: Many interpreters are freely accessible to run Python scripts, such as IDLE (Integrated Development Environment), which comes included with the Python software obtained at http://python.org/.

Linux: Python is included with mainstream Linux distributions such as Ubuntu and Fedora. In the terminal emulator, type "python" to see the version of Python you're using. The interpreter should launch and display the version number.

macOS: Python 2.7 is often included with macOS. Python 3 must be manually installed from http://python.org/.

## PYTHON INSTALLATION ON LINUX

Every Linux system, includes the following operating systems,

- Ubuntu
- CentOS
- Debian
- Fedora
- openSUSE
- Linux Mint
- Arch Linux.

Python will already be installed. You may test it by typing the following command into the terminal.

**$ python --version**

To check the latest version of python 2.x.x :

**$ python2 --version**

To check the latest version of python 3.x.x :

**$ python3 –version**

It will not be the most recent version of Python. Python may be installed on a Linux base system in a variety of ways, depending on your Linux system. The following commands would very certainly work on any Linux machine.

$ sudo add-apt-repository ppa:deadsnakes/ppa

$ sudo apt-get update

$ sudo apt-get install python3.11.2

**Download and install Python's Latest Version on Linux**

Follow the instructions below to install the most recent version of Python from its source code:

Python's most recent version may be downloaded at python.org.

The first step is to open a browser and navigate to https://www.python.org/downloads/source/.

Under Stable Releases, locate Download Gzipped source tarball (the most recent stable release is Python 3.11.2).

**Download and install Homebrew Package Manager**

Follow the procedures below if you do not have homebrew installed on your machine. Open the macOS Terminal application by going to Application -> Utilities. The Bash terminal will open, allowing you to input commands.

In the macOS terminal, type /bin/bash -c "$(curl -fSSL https://raw.githubusercontent.com/Homebrew/install/HEAD/install.sh)"

If asked, enter the system password. This will install Homebrew package Manager on your operating system. After you see the "Installation Successful" notification. You are now ready to install Python 3 on your Mac.

To test the installation, run the following instructions in your Python Terminal window

pip3

Python is already installed on your system. You may learn more about Python by clicking here.

- Offline Python 3.11 interpreter: Python applications may be run without connecting to the Internet.
- Pip package management, as well as a unique repository for prebuilt wheel packages for advanced scientific libraries like numpy, scipy, matplotlib, and scikit-learn.
- Tensorflow is now available as well.
- Examples are accessible right now to help you learn faster.
- Tkinter GUI support is complete.
- Terminal Emulator with full readline capabilities (available in pip).
- Go to the Google Play Store to get the Pydroid app.

When the installation is finished, launch the program, and it will display that Python is being installed.

Wait a minute for the ide to appear. You may insert the Python code here. To run the code, click the yellow button.

Python has been successfully installed.

## PYTHON PROGRAMMING

More information is required before we can begin programming in Python. I.e., installing Python software and running a Python program or script. Python 2 and Python 3 are the two primary Python versions. Python 2 and Python 3 are very different. Python 3 is used in this course since it is more semantically accurate and offers newer capabilities. We can read or run Python scripts or programs after successfully installing Python software.

**Python provides two methods for running a python script:**

- Using a script file
- Using Interactive interpreter prompt

**Using Interactive interpreter prompt:**

Python allows us to run Python statements one by one at the interactive prompt. It is ideal when we are concerned with the output of each line of our Python application. To enter interactive mode, open the terminal (or command prompt) and type python (python3 if you have both python2 and python3 installed on your machine). Command Prompt:

```
C:\Windows\system32\cmd.exe - python
Microsoft Windows [Version 6.1.7601]
Copyright (c) 2009 Microsoft Corporation.  All rights reserved.

C:\Users\Madhu>python
Python 3.8.3 (tags/v3.8.3:6f8c832, May 13 2020, 22:20:19) [MSC v.1925 32 bit (In
tel)] on win32
Type "help", "copyright", "credits" or "license" for more information.
>>> print("Hello")
Hello
>>> print("Welcome to Python")
Welcome to Python
>>>
```

(or)

In Windows, look for Python IDLE in all programs and then click on it to launch the Python interpreter prompt.

This is how the Python interpreter prompt looks.

```
Python 3.8.3 Shell
File  Edit  Shell  Debug  Options  Window  Help
Python 3.8.3 (tags/v3.8.3:6f8c832, May 13 2020, 22:20:19) [MSC v.1925 32 bit (In
tel)] on win32
Type "help", "copyright", "credits" or "license()" for more information.
>>> print("Hello")
Hello
>>> print("Welcome to python")
Welcome to python
>>> a=10
>>> b=20
>>> a+b
30
>>>
```

**Using Script File:**

The interpreter prompt is useful for running the code's individual statements. However, if we want to run numerous Python commands at once rather than one by one, we may utilize a script file. We must save our script into a file that can be run later.

Open an editor such as notepad, create a file named filename.py (Python uses the.py extension), and write the Python script in it.

Python is the programming language that opens the most doors. With a thorough understanding of Python, you may work in a wide range of occupations and sectors. Even if you don't need it for work, knowing it will help you speed up some tasks or have a better knowledge of other ideas.

Python is an excellent programming language for careers in software development, engineering, DevOps, machine learning, data analytics, web development, and testing. Furthermore, Python is used in numerous occupations outside of the IT sector. Python has become a must-have tool in the toolbox of educators, managers, data scientists, data analysts, economists, psychologists, artists, and even secretaries as our lives become more computerized every day, and computer and technology areas previously associated only with technically gifted people are now opening up to non-programmers.

## INSTALLING PYCHARM: A PYTHON CODE EDITOR

**Here's a step-by-step guide to downloading and installing Pycharm IDE on Windows:**

Step 1: To download PyCharm, go to https://www.jetbrains.com/pycharm/download/ and select the "DOWNLOAD" option under the Community Section.

Step 2: When the download is finished, launch the exe to install PyCharm. The installation wizard should have begun. Next, press the "Next" button.

Step 3: Change the installation path if necessary on the following screen. Next, press the "Next" button.

Step 4: If you choose, you may create a desktop shortcut on the following screen before clicking "Next."

Step 5: Select the Start Menu folder. Keep JetBrains selected and press the "Install" button.

Step 6: Wait for the installation to complete.

Step 7: When the installation is complete, you should get a message screen indicating that PyCharm is now installed. If you want to run it right away, check the "Run PyCharm Community Edition" box first, then hit the "Finish" button.

Step 8: After you click "Finish," the screen below will appear.

# CHAPTER ONE: PYTHON FUNDAMENTALS

## PYTHON VARIABLES

Python variables is the memory addresses designated for storing values in a Python program. This implies that when you create a variable, you reserve memory space.

The Python interpreter allocates memory and chooses what can be put in the reserved memory based on the data type of a variable. As a result, by assigning multiple data types to Python variables, you may store integers, decimals, or characters.

## CREATING PYTHON VARIABLES

Python variables do not require explicit declaration in order to reserve memory space or to create a variable. When you gives a value to a Python variable, it is automatically generated. To give values to variables, use the equal symbol (=).

The variable's name is the operand to the left of the = operator, and the variable's value is the operand to the right of the = operator.

**As an example:**

```
counter = 100      # Creates an integer variable
miles   = 1000.0    # Creates a floating point variable
name    = "micheal mick"  # Creates a string variable
```

## PRINTING PYTHON VARIABLES

We may use the print() method to print a Python variable after we create it and give it a value. The following is an expansion of the preceding example that demonstrates how to print distinct variables in Python:

```
counter = 100      # Creates an integer variable
miles   = 1000.0    # Creates a floating point variable
name    = " micheal mick "   # Creates a string variable
print (counter)
print (miles)
print (name)
```

The values assigned to the counter, miles, and name variables are 100, 1000.0, and " micheal mick ", respectively. When the above Python program is run, the following result is obtained:

100

1000.0
micheal mick

## DELETE A VARIABLE

Using the del command, you may remove a reference to a number object. The del statement has the following syntax:
del var1[,var2[,var3[....,varN]]]]

Using the del statement, you may remove a single item or several objects.
del var
del var_a, var_b

**Example**
The following examples demonstrate how to remove a variable, and attempting to use a deleted variable will result in an error from the Python interpreter:
counter = 100
print (counter)
del counter
print (counter)
This will results in inthee following outcome:
100
Traceback (most recent call last):
  File "main.py", line 7, in <module>
  print (counter)
NameError: name 'counter' is not defined

## MULTIPLE ASSIGNMENTS

Python allows you to give a single value to several variables at the same time, which implies you can create numerous variables at the same time.
a = b = c = 100
print (a)
print (b)
print (c)
This produces the following outcome:
100
100
100
In this case, an integer object with the value 1 is formed, and all three variables are allocated to the same memory region. You may also assign different objects to different variables. As an example,

```
a,b,c = 1,2,"micheal mick"
print (a)
print (b)
print (c)
```
This produces the following outcome:
```
1
2
micheal mick
```
In this case, two integer objects with values 1 and 2 are allocated to variables a and b, while one string object with the value "micheal mick" is assigned to variabl

## PYTHON VARIABLE NAMES

Every Python variable should have a distinct name, such as a, b, or c. A variable name can be meaningful, such as color, age, or name. When naming a Python variable, the following guidelines should be followed:

- A variable name must begin with a letter or an underscore.
- A variable name cannot begin with a number or a special character such as $, (, *%, and so on.
- Only alphanumeric letters and underscores (A-z, 0-9, and _) are permitted in variable names.
- Because Python variable names are case-sensitive, Name and NAME are distinct variables.
- Python-reserved keywords cannot be used in variable names.

**Example**
The following are examples of proper Python variable names:
```
counter = 100
_count  = 100
name1 = "micheal"
name2 = "mick"
Age  = 28
zara_salary = 100000
print (counter)
print (_count)
print (name1)
print (name2)
print (Age)
print (micheal_salary)
```
This will result in the following outcome:

100
100
micheal
mick
28
100000
Example
The following are examples of incorrect Python variable names:
1counter = 100
$_count  = 100
micheal-salary = 100000
print (1counter)
print ($count)
print (micheal-salary
This will result in the following outcome:
File "main.py", line 3
    1counter = 100
       ^
SyntaxError: invalid syntax

## PYTHON LOCAL VARIABLE

Local variables in Python are declared within a function. We are unable to access variables outside of the function. Python functions are reusable pieces of code that you will learn more about in the Python - Functions lesson. The following is an example of how to use local variables:

```
def sum(x,y):
  sum = x + y
  return sum
print(sum(5, 10))
15
```

## PYTHON GLOBAL VARIABLE

Any variable defined outside of a function may be accessed from within any function, giving it global scope. Here's an example of a global variable:

```
x = 5
y = 10
def sum():
  sum = x + y
  return sum
```

print(sum())
This will result in the following outcome:
15

## RESERVED WORDS (KEYWORDS)

Another restriction applies to identifier names. The Python programming language has a tiny collection of reserved keywords that represent specific language capabilities. A reserved term cannot have the same name as an object. There are 33 reserved keywords in Python 3.6:

### Keywords

| | | | |
|---|---|---|---|
| False | def | if | raise |
| None | del | import | return |
| True | elif | in | try |
| and | else | is | while |
| as | except | lambda | with |
| assert | finally | nonlocal | yield |
| break | for | not | |
| class | from | or | |
| continue | global | pass | |

This list may be accessed at any moment by entering help("keywords") into the Python interpreter. Reserved terms must be used precisely as shown and are case-sensitive. Except for False, None, and True, they are all in lowercase. Attempting to create a variable with the same name as any reserved word yields the following error:

>>> for = 3
SyntaxError: invalid syntax

Using the code below, we can also obtain all of the keyword names.
Example: Python Keywords List
# Python code to demonstrate working of iskeyword()
# importing "keyword" for keyword operations
import keyword
# printing all keywords at once using "kwlist()"
print("The list of keywords is : ")
print(keyword.kwlist)
Output
The list of keywords is :

['False', 'None', 'True', 'and', 'as', 'assert', 'async', 'await', 'break', 'class', 'continue', 'def', 'del', 'elif', 'else', 'except', 'finally', 'for', 'from', 'global', 'if', 'import', 'in', 'is', 'lambda', 'nonlocal', 'not', 'or', 'pass', 'raise', 'return', 'try', 'while', 'with', 'yield']

Let's go through each term in depth with some solid instances.

**True, False, None**

True: This keyword is used to represent a boolean true. If a statement is true, "True" is printed.

False: This keyword is used to represent a boolean false. If a statement is false, "False" is printed.

None: This is a special constant used to denote a null value or a void. It's important to remember, 0, any empty container(e.g empty list) does not compute to None.

It is an object of its datatype – NoneType. It is not possible to create multiple None objects and can assign them to variables.

**Example: True, False, and None Keyword**

print(False == 0)
print(True == 1)
print(True + True + True)
print(True + False + False)
print(None == 0)
print(None == [])
Output
True
True
3
1
False
False

Truth Table for and

| A | B | A and B |
|---|---|---|
| True | True | True |
| True | False | False |
| False | True | False |
| False | False | False |

**and, or, not, in, is**

and: This a logical operator in python. "and" Return the first false value. If not found return last. The truth table for "and" is depicted below.

3 and 0 returns 0

3 and 10 returns 10

10 or 20 or 30 or 10 or 70 returns 10

The preceding phrases may be perplexing to a programmer coming from a language such as C, where logical operators always produce boolean values (0 or 1). The following are direct quotes from the Python documentation:

The expression x and y evaluates x first; if x is false, its value is returned; otherwise, y is evaluated and its result is returned.

The expression x or y evaluates x first; if x is true, its value is returned; otherwise, y is evaluated and its value is returned.

It is worth noting that neither and nor or limit the value and type they return to False and True, but rather return the most recently evaluated argument. If s is a string that should be replaced by a default value if it is empty, the expression s or 'foo' returns the appropriate value. Because not must generate a new value, it always returns a boolean result regardless of the type of its input (for example, not 'foo' yields False rather than ".")

Truth Table for or

| A | B | A or B |
|---|---|--------|
| True | True | True |
| True | False | True |
| False | True | True |
| False | False | False |

or: In Python, this is a logical operator. "or" Return the first True value encountered. If no matches are found, return last. The truth table for the word "or" is shown below.

3 or 0 returns 3
3 or 10 returns 3
0 or 0 or 3 or 10 or 0 returns 3
not: This logical operator inverts the truth value. The truth table for "not" is depicted below.
in: This keyword is used to check if a container contains a value. This keyword is also used to loop through the container.
is: This keyword is used to test object identity, i.e to check if both the objects take the same memory location or not.
Example: and, or, not, is and in keyword
# showing logical operation
# or (returns True)
print(True or False)
# showing logical operation
# and (returns False)
print(False and True)
# showing logical operation
# not (returns False)
print(not True)
# using "in" to check
if 's' in 'geeksforgeeks':

25

```python
 print("s is part of geeksforgeeks")
else:
 print("s is not part of geeksforgeeks")
# using "in" to loop through
for i in 'geeksforgeeks':
 print(i, end=" ")
print("\r")
# using is to check object identity
# string is immutable( cannot be changed once allocated)
# hence occupy same memory location
print(' ' is ' ')
# using is to check object identity
# dictionary is mutable( can be changed once allocated)
# hence occupy different memory location
print({} is {})
```
Output:
True
False
False
s is part of geeksforgeeks
g e e k s f o r g e e k s
True
False
Iteration Keywords – for, while, break, continue
for: This keyword is used to control flow and for looping.
while: Has a similar working like "for", used to control flow and for looping.
break: "break" is used to control the flow of the loop. The statement is used to break out of the loop and passes the control to the statement following immediately after loop.
continue: "continue" is also used to control the flow of code. The keyword skips the current iteration of the loop but does not end the loop.
Example: For, while, break, continue keyword
```python
# Using for loop
for i in range(10):
 print(i, end=" ")
 # break the loop as soon it sees 6
 if i == 6:
  break
print()
# loop from 1 to 10
```

•

```
i = 0
while i < 10:
 # If i is equals to 6,
 # continue to next iteration
 # without printing
 if i == 6:
  i += 1
  continue
 else:
  # otherwise print the value
  # of i
  print(i, end=" ")
 i += 1
```

Output

0 1 2 3 4 5 6

0 1 2 3 4 5 7 8 9

Conditional keywords – if, else, elif

if : It is a control statement for decision making. Truth expression forces control to go in "if" statement block.

else : It is a control statement for decision making. False expression forces control to go in "else" statement block.

elif : It is a control statement for decision making. It is short for "else if"

**Example: if, else, and elif keyword**

```
# Python program to illustrate if-elif-else ladder
#!/usr/bin/python
i = 20
if (i == 10):
    print("i is 10")
elif (i == 20):
    print("i is 20")
else:
    print("i is not present")
```

Output

i is 20

def

def keyword is used to declare user defined functions.

**Example: def keyword**

```
# def keyword
def fun():
    print("Inside Function")
fun()
```

27

Output
Inside Function
**Return Keywords – Return, Yield**
return : This keyword is used to return from the function.
yield : This keyword is used like return statement but is used to return a generator.
**Example: Return and Yield Keyword**
```python
# Return keyword
def fun():
  S = 0
  for i in range(10):
   S += i
  return S
print(fun())
# Yield Keyword
def fun():
  S = 0
  for i in range(10):
   S += i
   yield S
for i in fun():
  print(i)
```
Output
45
0
1
3
6
10
15
21
28
36
45

**class**
class keyword is used to declare user defined classes.
Example: Class Keyword

```python
# Python3 program to
# demonstrate instantiating
# a class


class Dog:

    # A simple class
    # attribute
    attr1 = "mammal"
    attr2 = "dog"

    # A sample method
    def fun(self):
        print("I'm a", self.attr1)
        print("I'm a", self.attr2)


# Driver code
# Object instantiation
Rodger = Dog()

# Accessing class attributes
# and method through objects
print(Rodger.attr1)
Rodger.fun()
```

28

Output
mammal
I'm a mammal
I'm a dog
With
with keyword is used to wrap the execution of block of code within methods defined by context manager. This keyword is not used much in day to day programming.
Example: With Keyword

```
# using with statement
with open('file_path', 'w') as file:
    file.write('hello world !')
```

as
as keyword is used to create the alias for the module imported. i.e giving a new name to the imported module. E.g import math as mymath.
Example: as Keyword

```
import math as gfg

print(gfg.factorial(5))
```

Output
120
pass
In Python, the null statement is encountered and nothing occurs; it is used to prevent indentation issues and as a placeholder.

Example:
Pass
Keyword

```
n = 10
for i in range(n):

    # pass can be used as placeholder
    # when code is to added later
    pass
```

ctorial

1(10))

```
# from keyword
print(factorial(10))
```

Lambda
Lambda keyword is used to

29

make inline returning functions with no statements allowed internally. Example: Lambda Keyword

```
# Lambda keyword
g = lambda x: x*x*x

print(g(7))
```

Output
343
Import, From
import : This statement is used to include a particular module into current program.

from : Generally used with import, from is used to import particular functionality from the module imported.

Example: Import, From Keyword
Output
3628800
3628800

**Exception Handling Keywords – try, except, raise, finally, and assert**

try : This keyword is used for exception handling, used to catch the errors in the code using the keyword except. Code in "try" block is checked, if there is any type of error, except block is executed.

except : As explained above, this works together with "try" to catch exceptions.

finally : No matter what is result of the "try" block, block termed "finally" is always executed.

raise: We can raise an exception explicitly with the raise keyword

assert: This function is used for debugging purposes. Usually used to check the correctness of code. If a statement is evaluated to be true, nothing happens, but when it is false, "AssertionError" is raised. One can also print a message with the error, separated by a comma.

```
# initializing number
a = 4
b = 0

# No exception Exception raised in try block
try:
    k = a//b  # raises divide by zero exception.
    print(k)

# handles zerodivision exception
except ZeroDivisionError:
    print("Can't divide by zero")

finally:
    # this block is always executed
    # regardless of exception generation.
    print('This is always executed')

# assert Keyword
# using assert to check for 0
print("The value of a / b is : ")
assert b != 0, "Divide by 0 error"
print(a / b)

# raise keyword
# Raises an user defined exception
# if strings are not equal
temp = "geeks for geeks"
if temp != "geeks":
    raise TypeError("Both the strings are different.")
```

Example: try, except, raise, finally, and assert Keywords

Output
Can't divide by zero
This is always executed

The value of a / b is :
AssertionError : Divide by 0

```
# raise keyword
# Raises an user defined exception
# if strings are not equal
temp = "geeks for geeks"
if temp != "geeks":
    raise TypeError("Both the strings are different.")
```

error
Output
TypeError: Both the strings are different.
del
del is used to delete a reference to an object. Any variable or list value can be deleted using del.
Example: del Keyword
my_variable1 = 20
my_variable2 = "michealmick"
# check if my_variable1 and my_variable2 exists
print(my_variable1)
print(my_variable2)
# delete both the variables
del my_variable1
del my_variable2
# check if my_variable1 and my_variable2 exists
print(my_variable1)
print(my_variable2)
Output
20
michealmick
NameError: name 'my_variable1' is not defined
Global, Nonlocal
global: This keyword is used to declare a variable within the function to have global scope.
Non-local: Like global, this keyword declares a variable to point to a variable outside the enclosing function in the case of nested functions.

Example: Global and nonlocal keywords

```
# global variable
a = 15
b = 10

# function to perform addition
def add():
    c = a + b
    print(c)

# calling a function
add()

# nonlocal keyword
def fun():
    var1 = 10

    def gun():
        # tell python explicitly that it
        # has to access var1 initialized
        # in fun on line 2
        # using the keyword nonlocal
        nonlocal var1

        var1 = var1 + 10
        print(var1)

    gun()
fun()
```

Output
25
20

## CHECKING IF A STRING IS A KEYWORD IN PYTHON

Python's language defines an inherent module called "keyword" that handles keyword-related activities. The method "iskeyword()" determines whether or not a string is a keyword. If a string is a keyword, it returns true; otherwise, it returns false.

```
# Instead of writing this massive Python code
# we can also code this in a different way
# Python code to demonstrate working of iskeyword()
# importing "keyword" for keyword operations
import keyword
# initializing strings for testing while putting them in an array
keys = ["for", "michealmick", "elif", "elseif", "nikhil",
    "assert", "shambhavi", "True", "False", "akshat", "akash", "break",
"ashty", "lambda", "suman", "try", "vaishnavi"]
for i in range(len(keys)):
    # checking which are keywords
    if keyword.iskeyword(keys[i]):
    print(keys[i] + " is python keyword")
```

```
else:
    print(keys[i] + " is not a python keyword")
```
Output
for is python keyword
michealmick is not a python keyword
elif is python keyword
elseif is not a python keyword
nikhil is not a python keyword
assert is python keyword
shambhavi is not a python keyword
True is not a Python keyword
False is not a python keyword
akshat is not a Python keyword
akash is not a python keyword
break is python keyword
ashty is not a python keyword
lambda is python keyword
suman is not a python keyword
try is python keyword
vaishnavi is not a python keyword

## PYTHON STATEMENTS
## OPERATORS AND FLOW CONTROL STATEMENTS

In the Python language, a statement refers to an instruction that can be executed by the Python interpreter. Python encompasses various types of statements, including assignment statements, conditional statements, and looping statements, among others. The token character "NEWLINE" is utilized to conclude a statement in Python, indicating that each line within a Python script represents a distinct statement. These statements collectively contribute to facilitating the attainment of desired output for the user.

In this chapter, we will delve into the fundamental concepts of operators and flow control statements in Python. Understanding these concepts is essential for writing efficient and effective Python programs. We will explore various types of operators, including arithmetic, assignment, comparison, and logical operators. Additionally, we will learn about flow control statements like conditional statements (if-else) and loops.

Operators allow us to perform calculations, assign values, and compare data, enabling us to manipulate variables effectively. Flow control statements provide us with the ability to make decisions and control the execution flow of our programs. By mastering these concepts, you will have a solid foundation for writing more complex and sophisticated Python programs.

## Types of Statements in Python?

### Operators

**Arithmetic Operators:**
Arithmetic operators allow us to perform mathematical computations. We will explore operators like addition (+), subtraction (-), multiplication (*), division (/), and modulus (%). We will learn how to use these operators to perform calculations with both integers and floating-point numbers. Additionally, we will discuss operator precedence and the use of parentheses to control the order of operations.

**Assignment Operators:**
Assignment operators are used to assign values to variables. We will explore the basic assignment operator (=) and delve into compound assignment operators like +=, -=, *=, /=, and %=, which allow us to combine an arithmetic operation with assignment in a concise manner. Furthermore, we will discover how to assign multiple values to multiple variables in a single line.

**Comparison Operators:**
Comparison operators enable us to compare values and determine their relationship. We will examine operators such as == (equal to), != (not equal to), > (greater than), < (less than), >= (greater than or equal to), and <= (less than or equal to). We will learn how to use these operators to create conditional expressions and make decisions in our code. We will also discuss chaining comparison operators to form more complex conditions.

**Logical Operators:**
Logical operators allow us to combine conditions and perform logical operations. We will explore the logical AND (and), OR (or), and NOT

(not) operators. By understanding these operators, we can construct complex conditions that involve multiple comparisons. We will also discuss short-circuit evaluation, truthiness, and falsiness, which are essential concepts when working with logical operators.

**Flow Control Statements**
Conditional Statements (if-else):
Conditional statements, such as if and else, enable us to make decisions in our code. We will learn how to use if statements to execute specific blocks of code based on conditions. We will also explore the elif (else if) statement, which allows us to handle multiple alternative conditions. Furthermore, we will discuss the else statement, which provides a fallback option when all other conditions fail.

**Loops:**
Loops allow us to repeat a block of code multiple times. We will cover two types of loops: the while loop and the for loop.

**While Loop:**
The while loop executes a block of code repeatedly as long as a condition remains true. We will learn how to set up the condition, execute the code block, and update the loop control variable. We will also explore the use of break and continue statements to control the flow of the loop and handle specific situations.

**For Loop:**
The for loop is used to iterate over a sequence or collection of items. We will learn how to use the range function to generate a sequence of numbers and iterate over it. We will explore looping through strings, lists, and other data structures, extracting and manipulating data as we iterate.

**Control Statements:**
In addition to the regular flow control statements, we will also discuss control statements like pass, break, and continue.

The pass statement is used as a placeholder when we want to create a code block with no action.
The break statement allows us to exit a loop prematurely, based on a certain condition.
The continue statement enables us to skip the current iteration of a loop and proceed to the next iteration.

**The following are the many types of Python statements:**
Statements with Multiple Lines
Conditional and Loop Statements in Python

- Python If-else
- Python for loop
- Python while loop
- Python try-except
- Python with statement

Python Expression statements

- Python pass statement
- Python del statement
- Python return statement
- Python import statement
- Python continue and
- Python break statement

Example:
Parentheses (), braces (), square brackets [], semi-colon (;), and continuation character slash () can be used to extend a Python statement to one or more lines when the programmer wants to conduct extensive computations and cannot fit his instructions into one line.
Declared using Continuation Character (\):
s = 1 + 2 + 3 + \
    4 + 5 + 6 + \
    7 + 8 + 9
Declared using parentheses () :
n = (1 * 2 * 3 + 7 + 8 + 9)
Declared using square brackets [] :
footballer = ['RONALDO',
        'KANE,
        'MESSI']
Declared using braces {} :
x = {1 + 2 + 3 + 4 + 5 + 6 +
    7 + 8 + 9}
Declared using semicolons(;) :
flag = 2; ropes = 3; pole = 4

# PYTHON INDENTATION

In Python, whitespace is utilized for indentation. Python indentation is required, unlike many other programming languages, which just help to make the code simpler to read. An example of indentation in Python might help one grasp it better.

**Role of Indentation in Python**

A block is made up of all of these statements. A block is a collection of sentences that have a certain function. Braces are used to define a block of code for indentation in most programming languages, including C, C++, and Java. Python's use of indentation to emphasize code chunks is one of its distinguishing features. All statements with the same distance to the right are part of the same code block. If a block has to be nested further, it is simply indented farther to the right.

Example 1:

Print('Logging in to michealmick...') and print('retype the URL.') are two distinct code pieces. In our example if-statement, the two sections of code are both indented four spaces. Because the final print ('All set!') is not indented, it is not part of the else-block.

```
# Python indentation
site = 'gfg'
if site == 'gfg':
 print('Logging on to michealmick...')
else:
 print('retype the URL.')
print('All set !')
```

Output

Logging on to michealmick...

All set !

Example 2:

In Python, you must indent each line of code by the same amount of whitespace to denote a block of code. The while loop's two lines of code are both indented four spaces. It is needed to indicate which code block a statement belongs to. For instance, j=1 and while(j=5): are not indented and hence do not fall within the while block. Indentation is used to organise Python code.

Output: 1 2 3 4 5

## PYTHON COMMENTS

Python comments begin with the hash symbol # and extend all the way to the end of the line. Comments in Python are helpful information provided by developers to help the reader comprehend the source code. It describes the reasoning, or a portion of it, that is employed in the code.

When you are no longer available to answer queries about your code, comments in Python are frequently useful to someone who is maintaining or improving it. These is frequently touted as good programming conventions that do not affect program output but increase overall readability. In Python, comments are denoted by the hash symbol # and extend to the end of the line.

### TYPES OF COMMENTS IN PYTHON

A remark can be written on a single line, adjacent to a line of code, or in a block of numerous lines. Here, we'll go over some Python comment examples one by one:

**Single-line comment in Python**

Python single-line comments begin with a hash symbol (#) and continue to the end of the line. If the comment is longer than one line, add a hashtag to the following line and continue the comment. Single-line comments in Python have proven beneficial for providing quick explanations for variables, function declarations, and expressions. See the following code snippet for an example of an one line comment:

Example 1:

Python enables comments at the beginning of lines, and the entire line is ignored.

```
# This is a comment
# Print "michealmick" to console
print("michealmick")
```

Output

michealmick

Example 2:

Python also supports comments at the end of lines, which ignore the preceding text.

```
a, b = 1, 3   # Declaring two integers
sum = a + b   # adding two integers
print(sum)  # displaying the output
```

Output

4

Multiline comment in Python

To make a multiline remark, use a hash (#) for each extra line. In truth, Python's syntax does not support multiline comments. We can also utilize Python multi-line comments by utilizing multiline strings. It is a chunk of text with a delimiter (""") at each end of the comment. Again, no white space should exist between the delimiter ("""). They are useful when the remark content does not fit on a single line and must spread across lines. Python multi-line comments or paragraphs serve as documentation for other programmers who read your work. See the following code snippet for an example of a multi-line comment:

Example 1:

To generate a Python multiline comment, we need one additional # for each extra line in this example.

```
# This is a comment
# This is second comment
# Print "michealmick" to console
print("michealmick ")
Output
Michealmick
```

Example 2:

To generate a Python multiline comment, we use three double quotes (") at the beginning and end of the text without any space.

```
"""
This would be a multiline comment in Python that spans several lines and describes Michealmick.
A Computer Science portal for Micheal. It contains well written, well thought and well-explained computer science
and programming articles,
quizzes and more.
...
"""
print("Michealmick")
Output
Michealmick
```

Example 3:

To generate a Python multiline comment, we use three single quotes (') at the beginning and end of the text

```
# program illustrates the use of docstrings

def helloWorld():
    # This is a docstring comment
    """ This program prints out hello world """
    print("Hello World")


helloWorld()
```

without any space.
'''This article on geeksforgeeks gives you a
perfect example of
multi-line comments'''
print("Michealmick")
Output
Michealmick

## PYTHON DOCSTRING

Python Docstrings are a form of remark used to demonstrate how the program works. Python Docstrings are wrapped by Triple Quotes (""" """). The interpreter also ignores docstrings.
Output
Hello World

## DIFFERENCES BETWEEN 'DOCSTRINGS' AND 'MULTI-LINE COMMENTS'

Docstrings and multi-line comments may appear to be the same thing, but they are not.

* Docstrings are used in functions and classes to demonstrate how to utilize the program.
* Multi-line comments are used to demonstrate how a section of code works.

## WHITE SPACES

*The following are the most prevalent whitespace characters:*

| Character | ASCII Code | Literal Expression |
|-----------|------------|--------------------|
| Space | 32 (0x20) | ' ' |
| tab | 9 (0x9) | '\t' |
| newline | 10 (0xA) | '\n' |

The Python interpreter mainly ignores and does not need whitespace.

Whitespace can be eliminated when it is evident where one token finishes and the next one begins. When special non-alphanumeric characters are included, this is frequently the case.

Examples:

```
# Example 1

# This is correct but whitespace can improve readability

a = 1-2   # Better way is a = 1 - 2

print(a)


# Example 2

# This is correct
# Whitespace here can improve readability.
x = 10
flag =(x == 10)and(x<12)
print(flag)

""" Readable form could be as follows
x = 10
flag = (x == 10) and (x < 12)
print(flag)
"""

# Try the more readable code yourself
```

Whitespaces are required to separate keywords from variables or other keywords. Consider the following scenario.

```
# Example

x = [1, 2, 3]
y = 2

""" Following is incorrect, and will generate syntax error
a = yin x
"""

# Corrected version is written as
a = y in x
print(a)
```

## WHITESPACES AS INDENTATION

Python's syntax is simple, but you must exercise caution while creating code. Python code is written with indentation. Whitespaces preceding a statement play an important function in indentation. The significance of whitespace preceding a sentence might vary. Let's look at an example.

```
# Example

print('foo') # Correct

   print('foo') # This will generate an error

# The error would be somewhat 'unexpected indent'
```

```
# Example

x = 10

while(x != 0):
  if(x > 5):    # Line 1
    print('x > 5')  # Line 2
  else:        # Line 3
    print('x < 5') # Line 4
  x -= 2       # Line 5

" " "
Lines 1, 3, 5 are on same level
Line 2 will only be executed if if condition becomes true.
Line 4 will only be executed if if condition becomes false.
" " "
```

Leading whitespaces are used to group statements together, such as in loops or control structures.

Example:
Output:
x > 5
x > 5
x > 5
x < 5

x < 5

## PACKING AND UNPACKING ARGUMENTS IN PYTHON

We use two operators * (for tuples) and ** (for dictionaries).

**Background**

Consider the following scenario: we have a function that takes four arguments. We wish to call this function, and we have a list of size 4 containing all of the function's parameters. The call fails if we merely send a list to the function.

```
# A Python program to demonstrate need
# of packing and unpacking

# A sample function that takes 4 arguments
# and prints them.
def fun(a, b, c, d):
    print(a, b, c, d)

# Driver Code
my_list = [1, 2, 3, 4]

# This doesn't work
fun(my_list)
```

Output :
TypeError: fun() takes exactly 4 arguments (1 given)

## UNPACKING

We can use * to unpack the list so that all elements of it can be passed as different parameters.

```
# A sample function that takes 4 arguments
# and prints the,
def fun(a, b, c, d):
    print(a, b, c, d)

# Driver Code
my_list = [1, 2, 3, 4]

# Unpacking list into four arguments
fun(*my_list)
```

Output :
(1, 2, 3, 4)

We must remember that the number of arguments must be equal to the length of the list that we are unpacking for the arguments.

```
# Error when len(args) != no of actual arguments
# required by the function

args = [0, 1, 4, 9]


def func(a, b, c):
    return a + b + c


# calling function with unpacking args
func(*args)
```

Output:
Traceback (most recent call last):
  File "/home/592a8d2a568a0c12061950aa99d6dec3.py", line 10, in <module>
    func(*args)
TypeError: func() takes 3 positional arguments but 4 were given

Consider the built-in range() method, which requires distinct start and finish inputs. If they are not accessible separately, use the *-operator in the function call to unpack the parameters from a list or tuple:

```
>>>
>>> range(3, 6)  # normal call with separate arguments
[3, 4, 5]
>>> args = [3, 6]
>>> range(*args)  # call with arguments unpacked from a list
[3, 4, 5]
```

## PACKING

When we don't know how many parameters to send to a Python method, we may use Packing to concatenate all arguments into a tuple.

```
# A Python program to demonstrate use
# of packing

# This function uses packing to sum
# unknown number of arguments
def mySum(*args):
    return sum(args)

# Driver code
print(mySum(1, 2, 3, 4, 5))
print(mySum(10, 20))
```

Output:
15
30

The preceding function mySum() uses 'packing' to combine all of the inputs received by this method call into a single variable. Once we have this 'packed' variable, we may use it in the same way as we would a regular tuple. The first and second arguments would be returned by args[0] and args[1, respectively. Because our tuples are immutable, you may transform the args tuple to a list and change, remove, and rearrange the elements in i.

## PACKING AND UNPACKING

Below is an example that shows both packing and unpacking.
# A Python program to demonstrate both packing and
# unpacking.
# A sample python function that takes three arguments
# and prints them
    def fun1(a, b, c):
    print(a, b, c)
# Another sample function.
# This is an example of PACKING. All arguments passed
# to fun2 are packed into tuple *args.
def fun2(*args):
 # Convert args tuple to a list so we can modify it

44

```
args = list(args)
    # Modifying args
    args[0] = 'Michealmick'
    args[1] = 'awesome'
# UNPACKING args and calling fun1()
fun1(*args)
# Driver code
fun2('Hello', 'beautiful', 'world!')
```
Output:
(Michealmick, awesome, world!)
The time complexity of the given Python program is O(1), which means it does not depend on the size of the input. The auxiliary space complexity of the program is O(n), where n is the number of arguments passed to the fun2 function.

** is used for dictionaries

```
# A sample program to demonstrate unpacking of
# dictionary items using **
def fun(a, b, c):
    print(a, b, c)

# A call with unpacking of dictionary
d = {'a':2, 'b':4, 'c':10}
fun(**d)
```

Output:
2 4 10
Here ** unpacked the dictionary used with it, and passed the items in the dictionary as keyword arguments to the function. So writing "fun(1, **d)" was equivalent to writing "fun(1, b=4, c=10)".

```
# A Python program to demonstrate packing of
# dictionary items using **
def fun(**kwargs):
    # kwargs is a dict
    print(type(kwargs))
        # Printing dictionary items
        for key in kwargs:
            print("%s = %s" % (key, kwargs[key]))
# Driver code
fun(name="micheal", ID="101", language="Python")
```
Output
```
<class 'dict'>
name = micheal
ID = 101
language = Python
```

## EXERCISES

You now know a lot about variables and how to utilize them in Python. Are you prepared to take a test? To make the code operate as anticipated, try inserting the missing part:
Exercise:
Create a variable named socialmedia and assign the value facebook to it.
Answer

## TYPE CONVERSION IN PYTHON

Python includes type conversion routines that allow you to directly convert one data type to another, which is important in both every day and competitive programming. This page will provide information on various conversion functions. In Python, there are two forms of type conversion:

* Implicit Type Conversion
* Explicit Type Conversion

## IMPLICIT TYPE CONVERSION

The Python interpreter automatically changes one data type to another through implicit type conversion without user intervention. See the examples below for a better understanding of the subject.
Example:

```
x = 10
print("x is of type:",type(x))

y = 10.6
print("y is of type:",type(y))

z = x + y

print(z)
print("z is of type:",type(z))
```

Output:
x is of type: <class 'int'>
y is of type: <class 'float'>
20.6
z is of type: <class 'float'>
As we can see, the data type of 'z' was automatically transformed to "float" although one variable x is integer and the other variable y is float. The float value is not changed into an integer because of type promotion, which allows operations to be performed by changing data into a larger-sized data type without losing information. This is a basic example of Python's Implicit type conversion.

## EXPLICIT TYPE CONVERSION

The data type in Python is explicitly updated by the user as needed in Explicit Type Conversion. Because we are forcing an expression to be altered in some specified data type, there is a danger of data loss with explicit type conversion. The following are some examples of explicit type conversion:

1. int(a, base): This function converts any data type to integer. 'Base' specifies the base in which string is if the data type is a string.
2. float(): This function is used to convert any data type to a floating-point number.

```
# Python code to demonstrate Type conversion
# using int(), float()

# initializing string
s = "10010"

# printing string converting to int base 2
c = int(s,2)
print ("After converting to integer base 2 : ", end="")
print (c)

# printing string converting to float
e = float(s)
print ("After converting to float : ", end="")
print (e)
```

Output:
After converting to integer base 2 : 18
After converting to float : 10010.0

3. ord() : This function is used to convert a character to integer.
4. hex() : This function is to convert integer to hexadecimal string.
5. oct() : This function is to convert integer to octal string.

```
# Python code to demonstrate Type conversion
# using ord(), hex(), oct()

# initializing integer
s = '4'

# printing character converting to integer
c = ord(s)
print ("After converting character to integer : ",end="")
print (c)

# printing integer converting to hexadecimal string
c = hex(56)
print ("After converting 56 to hexadecimal string : ",end="")
print (c)

# printing integer converting to octal string
c = oct(56)
print ("After converting 56 to octal string : ",end="")
print (c)
```

Output:
After converting character to integer : 52
After converting 56 to hexadecimal string : 0x38
After converting 56 to octal string : 0o70

6. tuple() : This function is used to convert to a tuple.
7. set() : This function returns the type after converting to set.
8. list() : This function is used to convert any data type to a list type.

```
# Python code to demonstrate Type conversion
# using tuple(), set(), list()

# initializing string
s = 'geeks'

# printing string converting to tuple
c = tuple(s)
print ("After converting string to tuple : ",end="")
print (c)

# printing string converting to set
c = set(s)
print ("After converting string to set : ",end="")
print (c)

# printing string converting to list
c = list(s)
print ("After converting string to list : ",end="")
print (c)
```

Output:
After converting string to tuple : ('g', 'e', 'e', 'k', 's')
After converting string to set : {'k', 'e', 's', 'g'}
After converting string to list : ['g', 'e', 'e', 'k', 's']

9. dict() : This function is used to convert a tuple of order (key,value) into a dictionary.
10. str() : Used to convert integer into a string.
11. complex(real,imag) : This function converts real numbers to complex(real,imag) number.

```
# Python code to demonstrate Type conversion
# using dict(), complex(), str()

# initializing integers
a = 1
b = 2

# initializing tuple
tup = (('a', 1) ,('f', 2), ('g', 3))

# printing integer converting to complex number
c = complex(1,2)
print ("After converting integer to complex number : ",end="")
print (c)

# printing integer converting to string
c = str(a)
print ("After converting integer to string : ",end="")
print (c)

# printing tuple converting to expression dictionary
c = dict(tup)
print ("After converting tuple to dictionary : ",end="")
print (c)
```

Output:
After converting integer to complex number : (1+2j)
After converting integer to string : 1
After converting tuple to dictionary : {'a': 1, 'f': 2, 'g': 3}

12. chr(number): This function converts number to its corresponding ASCII character.

```
# Convert ASCII value to characters
a = chr(76)
b = chr(77)

print(a)
print(b)
```

Output:
L
M

## NAMESPACE

A namespace in Python serves as a distinct system where each object is assigned a unique name. Objects can take the form of variables or methods. Python employs its own namespace in the form of a dictionary. Let's delve into an analogy to comprehend this better—an analogy drawn from the structure of a directory-file system found in computers.

Naturally, multiple directories can contain files sharing the same name. However, by specifying the absolute path, one can precisely navigate to the desired file. Consider this real-time example: a namespace is akin to a surname. In a class, there might be several individuals named "Alice," yet if you specify "Alice Lee" or "Alice Clark" (including the surname), only one will be singled out (for now, let's not consider scenarios where multiple students share both the first name and surname).

Along the same lines, the Python interpreter discerns the exact method or variable being referenced in the code, based on the namespace.

The division of the term itself provides additional insights. It comprises "Name" (which signifies a unique identifier) and "Space" (which conveys something related to scope). Here, a name can represents any Python method or variable, while space depends on the location from which a variable or method is accessed.

## TYPES OF NAMESPACES

When the Python interpreter runs on its own, without any user-defined modules, methods, or classes, it includes a set of pre-existing functions such as print() and id(). These functions form part of the built-in namespace.

When a user creates a module, a global namespace is established. Subsequently, when local functions are created within the module, a local namespace is formed. It's important to note that the built-in namespace encompasses the global namespace, and the global namespace, in turn, encompasses the local namespace.

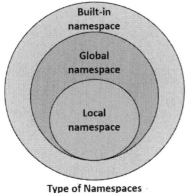

Type of Namespaces

**The lifetime of a namespace:**
The lifespan of a namespace is determined by the scope of its objects. When the scope of an object concludes, the namespace associated with it ceases to exist. Consequently, it is not feasible to access objects within an inner namespace from an outer namespace.
Example:

```
# var1 is in the global namespace
var1 = 5
def some_func():

    # var2 is in the local namespace
    var2 = 6
    def some_inner_func():

        # var3 is in the nested local
        # namespace
        var3 = 7
```

As seen in the graphic below, the same object name can exist in different namespaces since its namespace maintains isolation.

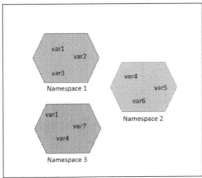

In certain situations, there may be a need to specifically update or process global variables. In the provided example, it is essential to explicitly declare the variable as global in order to modify or manipulate its value.
For instance, consider the line "count = count + 1" which

50

references the global variable and utilizes its current value for the operation.

However, if the line were written as "count = 1", it would no longer reference the global variable. In such cases, the line "global count" becomes necessary, following the rules of variable scope, to ensure that the global variable is accessed and modified appropriately.

```
# Python program processing
# global variable

count = 5
def some_method():
    global count
    count = count + 1
    print(count)
some_method()
```

Output: 6

## SCOPE OF OBJECTS IN PYTHON

The scope of a Python object is the coding region from which it may be accessed. As a result, one cannot access any particular object from anywhere in the code; access must be permitted by the object's scope. Let's look at an example to get a better understanding:

Example 1:

```
# Python program showing
# a scope of object

def some_func():
    print("Inside some_func")
    def some_inner_func():
        var = 10
        print("Inside inner function, value of var:",var)
    some_inner_func()
    print("Try printing var from outer function: ",var)
some_func()
```

Output:
Inside some_func
Inside inner function, value of var: 10
Traceback (most recent call last):
  File "/home/1eb47bb3eac2fa36d6bfe5d349dfcb84.py", line 8, in
    some_func()
  File "/home/1eb47bb3eac2fa36d6bfe5d349dfcb84.py", line 7, in some_func
    print("Try printing var from outer function: ",var)
NameError: name 'var' is not defined

51

# CHAPTER TWO: UNDERSTANDING PYTHON (INPUT AND OUTPUT)
## INPUT IN PYTHON

Developers frequently requires interaction with users, either to obtain data or to present results. In modern programming, dialog boxes are commonly used to prompt users for input. Python offers two built-in functions that enable reading input from the keyboard.

input ( prompt )

raw_input ( prompt )

input ():

The mentioned function receives input from the user and converts it into a string data type. The returned object will always be of the class 'str'. It does not evaluate the expression provided by the user; rather, it simply returns the entire input as a string. A specific example is the built-in function in Python called input(). What this function is called, it pauses the program's execution and waits for for user input. Once the user presses the enter key, the program resumes and returns the text that the user entered as a string.

Syntax:

inp = input('STATEMENT')

Example:

1.  >>> name = input('What is your name?\n')      # \n ---> newline  ---> It causes a line break

>>> What is your name?

     Ram

>>> print(name)

     Ram

     # ---> comment in python

```
# Python program showing
# a use of input()

val = input("Enter your value: ")
print(val)
```

Output:
```
Enter your value: 123
123
>>>
```

Taking String as an input:

```
name = input('What is your name?\n')     # \n ---> newline  ---> It causes a line break
print(name)
```

Output:
What is your name?
Ram
Ram

## HOW THE INPUT FUNCTION WORKS IN PYTHON

When the input() function is executed, the program flow will pause until the user provides input. The prompt, which is the text or message displayed on the output screen to request user input, is optional. The input() function converts whatever is entered by the user into a string, regardless of whether it is an integer or another type of value. If you want to treat the input as an integer in your code, you need to explicitly convert it using typecasting.

Code:

```
# Program to check input
# type in Python

num = input ("Enter number :")
print(num)
name1 = input("Enter name : ")
print(name1)

# Printing type of input value
print ("type of number", type(num))
print ("type of name", type(name1))
```

Output:
```
Enter number :123
123
Enter name :
'
type or number <class 'str'>
type of name <class 'str'>
>>> |
```

raw_input():The function mentioned in the statement is applicable to older versions of Python, such as Python 2.x. This function captures the exact input provided by the user through the keyboard, converts it into a string, and returns it to the specified variable for storage.

Example:

```
# Python program showing
# a use of raw_input()


g = raw_input("Enter your name : ")
print g
```

Output:
Enter your name : micheal
Micheal
>>>

In this context, the variable 'g' is used to store the string value entered by the user during the program's execution. The input data for the raw_input() function is concluded by pressing the enter key. It is possible to input numeric data using

53

raw_input() as well, but in such cases, typecasting is necessary to convert the input to the desired data type. For more information on typecasting, you can refer to relevant resources.

It is important to note that the input() function in Python captures all input as a string by default. There are various other functions available for receiving input in different formats. Some examples include:

- int(input())
- float(input())

```
num = int(input("Enter a number: "))
print(num, " ", type(num))
```

```
floatNum = float(input("Enter a decimal number: "))
print(floatNum, " ", type(floatNum))
```

Output:

```
Enter a number:
29     <class 'int'>
Enter a decimal number:
100.4   <class 'float'>
```

## INPUT FROM THE CONSOLE IN PYTHON

The Python Console, often referred to as the Shell, serves as a command line interpreter, processing user input command by command. Its primary function involves interpreting and executing commands provided by the user. In the absence of errors, the Console executes the command and delivers the desired output. However, when errors occur, it promptly displays error messages. A visual representation of the Python Console is presented below, illustrating its distinctive appearance.

```
File Edit Shell Debug Options Window Help
Python 3.6.4 (v3.6.4:d48eceb, Dec 19 2017, 06:54:40) [MSC v.1900
Type "copyright", "credits" or "license()" for more information.
>>> |
```

To executes a command in the Python console, simply type the command and press the Enter key. Upon pressing Enter, the console will interpret and execute the command. It is essential to have a basic understanding of the Python console when coding in Python. The primary prompt in the Python console is represented by three greater than symbols (>>>).

```
>>>
```

After executing the first command and seeing the prompts appear, you are then free to write the next command directly on the Python Console shell. The Python Console accepts commands written in the Python language that you input after the prompt.

```
Type "copyright", "credits"
>>> "hii everyone"
'hii everyone'
>>> |
```

To receive input from the user via the console, you can utilize the built-in function input(). This function allows the user to enter values directly into the console, which can then be utilized within the program as required. By using the input() function, you can prompt the user for specific information and store their input for further processing within your program.

```
# input
input1 = input()

# output
print(input1)
```

By defining the input() function inside the type, we may typecast this input to integer, float, or string.

## 1. Typecasting the input to Integer:

There may be times when you need integer input from the user/console; the following code accepts two integer/float inputs from the console and typecasts them to integers before printing the total.

```
# input
num1 = int(input())
num2 = int(input())

# printing the sum in integer
print(num1 + num2)
```

convert the input to a float.

## 2. Typecasting the input to Float:

The following code will

```
# input
num1 = float(input())
num2 = float(input())

# printing the sum in float
print(num1 + num2)
```

- **Typecasting the input to String:**

All types of input, whether float or integer, may be converted to string. For typecasting, we utilize the term str. We may also take an input string by simply writing input() function, which by default creates an input string.

```
# input
string = str(input())

# output
print(string)

# Or by default
string_default = input()

# output
print(string_default)
```

### TAKING MULTIPLE INPUTS FROM THE USER

The developer frequently requests that a user submit several numbers or inputs on a single line. In C++/C, many inputs may be taken in one line using scanf, while in Python, multiple values or inputs can be taken in one line using two techniques.

- Using split() method
- Using List comprehension

Using split() method :
The following utility facilitates the acquisition of multiple user inputs by segmenting the provided input using a designated separator. In the absence of a specified separator, any whitespace is considered as a separator. While the conventional approach for splitting a Python string involves the use of the split() method, this function enables the handling of multiple inputs as well.
Syntax :
input().split(separator, maxsplit)
Example:

```
# Python program showing how to
# multiple input using split

# taking two inputs at a time
x, y = input("Enter two values: ").split()
print("Number of boys: ", x)
print("Number of girls: ", y)

# taking three inputs at a time
x, y, z = input("Enter three values: ").split()
print("Total number of students: ", x)
print("Number of boys is : ", y)
print("Number of girls is : ", z)

# taking two inputs at a time
a, b = input("Enter two values: ").split()
print("First number is {} and second number is {}".format(a, b))

# taking multiple inputs at a time
# and type casting using list() function
x = list(map(int, input("Enter multiple values: ").split()))
print("List of students: ", x)
```

Output:
Enter two values: 5 10
Number of boys:  5
Number of girls:  10
Enter three values: 5 10 15
Total number of students:  5
Number of boys is :  10
Number of girls is :  15
Enter two values: 5 10
First number is 5 and second number is 10
Enter multiple values: 5 10 15 20 25
List of students:  [5, 10, 15, 20, 25]

## Using List comprehension :

```
# Python program showing
# how to take multiple input
# using List comprehension

# taking two input at a time
x, y = [int(x) for x in input("Enter two values: ").split()]
print("First Number is: ", x)
print("Second Number is: ", y)

# taking three input at a time
x, y, z = [int(x) for x in input("Enter three values: ").split()]
print("First Number is: ", x)
print("Second Number is: ", y)
print("Third Number is: ", z)

# taking two inputs at a time
x, y = [int(x) for x in input("Enter two values: ").split()]
print("First number is {} and second number is {}".format(x, y))

# taking multiple inputs at a time
x = [int(x) for x in input("Enter multiple values: ").split()]
print("Number of list is: ", x)
```

List comprehension is a sophisticated technique in Python for succinctly defining and generating lists. It allows us to create lists in a concise manner, akin to mathematical statements, all within a single line of code. Furthermore, list comprehension proves to be valuable when obtaining multiple inputs from users.

Example:

Output :
Enter two values: 5 10
First Number is:  5
Second Number is:  10
Enter three values: 5 10 15
First Number is:  5
Second Number is:  10
Third Number is:  15
Enter two values: 5 10
First number is 5 and second number is 10
Enter multiple values: 5 10 15 20 25
Number of list is:  [5, 10, 15, 20, 25]
Note: The preceding examples accept input separated by spaces. If we want to take input separated by commas (,), we may do it as follows:

```
# taking multiple inputs at a time separated by comma
x = [int(x) for x in input("Enter multiple value: ").split(",")]
print("Number of list is: ", x)
```

## OUTPUT IN PYTHON
## OUTPUT USING PRINT() FUNCTION

Python print() function prints the message to the screen or any other standard output device.
Syntax:
print(value(s), sep=' ', end = '\n', file=file, flush=flush)
Parameters:

- value(s): Any value, and as many as you like. Will be converted to a string before printed
- sep='separator' : (Optional) Specify how to separate the objects, if there is more than one.Default :' '
- end='end': (Optional) Specify what to print at the end.Default : '\n'
- file : (Optional) An object with a write method. Default :sys.stdout

- flush : (Optional) A Boolean, specifying if the output is flushed (True) or buffered (False). Default: False

**Return Type: It returns output to the screen.**
While it is not mandatory to provide arguments to the print() function, an empty set of parentheses must be included at the end to signal Python to execute the function rather than just referring to it by its name. Now, let us delve into the realm of optional arguments that can be employed with the print() function.

**String Literals**
In Python, string literals within the print statement serve a key purpose of formatting or styling the desired appearance of a particular string when it is printed using the print() function.
\n : This string literal is used to add a new blank line while printing a statement.
"" : An empty quote ("") is used to print an empty line.

Example:
print("Micheal \n is best for DSA Content.")
Output:
Micheal
is best for DSA Content.

```
# This line will automatically add a new line before the
# next print statement
print ("micheal is the best platform for DSA content")

# This print() function ends with "**" as set in the end argument.
print ("micheal is the best platform for DSA content", end= "**")
print("Welcome to GFG")
```

end= " " statement The "end" keyword is utilized to designate the content that will be printed at the conclusion of executing the print() function. By default, it is set to "\n", causing a line break to occur after the execution of the print() statement.
Example: Python print() without new line
Output:
Micheal is the best platform for DSA content
Micheal is the best platform for DSA content**Welcome to GFG
Flush Argument
In Python, input/output operations (I/Os) are typically buffered, meaning they are processed in chunks rather than individual elements. This is where the "flush" parameter becomes relevant, as it allows users to determine whether the written content should be buffered or not. By default, the flush

parameter is set to false. However, if set to true, the output will be written as a sequence of characters one after another. It's worth noting that this process can be slower since writing in chunks is more efficient than writing one character at a time. To grasp the practical application of the flush argument in the print() function, let's consider an example.

Example:

Assume you're creating a countdown timer that adds the remaining time to the same line every second. It would resemble the following:

3>>>2>>>1>>>Start

The original code for this might look something like this:

```
import time

count_seconds = 3
for i in reversed(range(count_seconds + 1)):
    if i > 0:
        print(i, end='>>>')
        time.sleep(1)
    else:
        print('Start')
```

As a result, the preceding code inserts text without a trailing newline and then sleeps for one second after each text insertion. It prints Start and ends the line at the conclusion of the countdown. If you execute the code as is, it waits for 3 seconds before printing the complete text. This is a 3 second waste caused by text chunk buffering, as demonstrated below:

Buffering serves a function, but it might have unintended consequences, as seen above. The flush parameter is used with the print() method to address the same issue. Set the flush parameter to true to see the results again.

Output:
Separator

```
import time

count_seconds = 3
for i in reversed(range(count_seconds + 1)):
    if i > 0:
        print(i, end='>>>', flush = True)
        time.sleep(1)
    else:
        print('Start')
```

Any number of positional parameters can be sent to the print() method. The keyword argument "sep" is used to distinguish this positional parameters. Because sep, end, flush, and file are keyword arguments, their order has no effect on the outcome of the function.
Example:
Output:
12-12-2022
Example:
Positional arguments cannot follow keyword arguments. In the example below, positions 10, 20, and 30 are positional arguments, whereas sep=' -'is a keyword argument.
Output:
File "0b97e8c5-bacf-4e89-9ea3-c5510b916cdb.py", line 1
 print(10, 20, sep=' - ', 30
        ^

SyntaxError: positional argument follows keyword argument
File Argument
Contrary to common perception, the print() method does not display messages on the screen. These is handled by lower-level code levels that may read data (message) in bytes. The print() method acts as an interface between this levels delegating printing to a stream or file-like object. The print() method is by default tied to sys.stdout through the file parameter.

```
import io

# declare a dummy file
dummy_file = io.StringIO()

# add message to the dummy file
print('Hello micheal!!', file=dummy_file)

# get the value from dummy file
dummy_file.getvalue()
```

Example: Python print() to file

Output:
'Hello micheal!!\n'

Example: with print() function to write content directly to text file.

```
print('Welcome to michealmick Python world.!!', file=open('Testfile.txt', 'w'))
```

Output:
% nano Testfile.txt
-----------------------------------------------------------------------------------------
----
   UW PICO 5.09                                    File: Testfile.txt

Welcome to michealmick Python world.

| ^G Get Help | ^O WriteOut | ^R Read File | ^Y Prev Pg | ^K |
| Cut Text | ^C Cur Pos | | | |
| ^X Exit | ^J Justify | ^W Where is | ^V Next Pg | ^U |
| UnCut Text | ^T To Spell | | | |

Example : Using print() function in Python

```
# Python 3.x program showing
# how to print data on
# a screen

# One object is passed
print("michealmick")

x = 5
# Two objects are passed
print("x =", x)

# code for disabling the softspace feature
print('G', 'F', 'G', sep='')

# using end argument
print("Python", end='@')
print("michealmick")
```

Output:
Michealmick
x = 5
GFG

## HOW TO PRINT WITHOUT NEWLINE IN PYTHON?

When transitioning from C/C++ to Python, individuals often inquire about the process of printing multiple variables or statements without starting a new line. This is because the default behavior of the Python print() function is to conclude with a newline character. In Python, if you simply use print(a_variable), it will automatically move to the next line as per the predefined format.

For example:

```
print("micheal")
print("michealmic")
```

This will result in this:

Michea
miche
mich

However, there are situations when we do not want to go to the next line and instead wish to print on the same line. So, what can we do?

For Example:

Input : [micheal,michealmick]
Output : michealmichealmick
Input : a = [1, 2, 3, 4]
Output : 1 2 3 4

## PRINT WITHOUT NEWLINE IN PYTHON 3.X WITHOUT USING FOR LOOP

```
# Print without newline in Python 3.x without using for loop

l = [1, 2, 3, 4, 5, 6]

# using * symbol prints the list
# elements in a single line
print(*l)

#This code is contributed by anuragsingh1022
```

Output
1 2 3 4 5 6

**Print without newline Using Python sys module**

To use the sys module, first import it using the import keyword. Then, inside the sys module, use the stdout.write() function to output your strings. It is only applicable to string. A TypeError will be thrown if you supply a number or a list.

```
import sys
```

```
sys.stdout.write("michealmick ")
sys.stdout.write("is best website for coding!")
```

Output
michealmick is best website for coding!

### PYTHON END PARAMETER IN PRINT()

By default, the print() method in Python terminates with a new line. A C/C++ coder may be perplexed as to how to print without a new line. The print() method in Python has an argument named 'end'. This parameter's default value is 'n which represents the new line character.
Example 1:
Using this argument, we may terminate a print statement with any character/string.
\# ends the output with a space
print("Welcome to", end = ' ')
print("michealmick", end= ' ')
Output:
Welcome to michealmick
Example 2:
One more program to demonstrate the working of the end parameter.
\# ends the output with '@'
print("Python", end='@')
print("michealmick")
Output:
Python@michealmick
Example 3:
The print() function uses the sep parameter to separate the arguments and ends after the last argument.

```
print('G','F', sep='', end=' ')
print('G')
```

```
#\n provides new line after printing the year
print('09','12','2016', sep='-', end='\n')
```

Using end to concatenate strings:

```
print('Red','Green','Blue', sep=',', end='@')
print('michealmick')
```

64

In this example, we utilize the "end" parameter to combine two print() statements into a single line of output. By setting the end parameter to a space character (" "), the first print() statement is followed by a space, allowing the second print() statement to start on the same line. This parameter serves as a valuable tool within the print() function in Python, offering control over the formatting of output in diverse ways.

```
name = "Alice"
age = 30
print("My name is", name, "and I am", age, "years old.", end=" ")
print("Nice to meet you!")
```

Output
My name is Alice and I am 30 years old. Nice to meet you!

## SEP PARAMETER IN PRINT()

The separator between arguments in the print() function in Python is a space character (known as the "softspace" feature). However, this separator can be modified to any character, integer, or string according to to our preferences. This is accomplished using the 'sep' parameter, which is available in Python 3.x or later versions. The 'sep' parameter, not only allows customization of the separator but also aids in formatting the output strings in a desired manner.

```
#code for disabling the softspace feature
print('G','F','G', sep='')
```
•

```
#for formatting a date
print('09','12','2016', sep='-')
```

```
#another example
print('pratik','michealmick', sep='@')
```

The sep parameter when used with the end parameter it produces awesome results. Some examples by combining the sep and end parameters.

**Note:** Please change the language from Python to Python 3 in the online ide.

```
print('G','F', sep='', end='')
print('G')
#\n provides new line after printing the year
print('09','12','2016', sep='-', end='\n')

print('prtk','agarwal', sep='', end='@')
print('michealmick')
```

65

Go to your interactive python ide by typing python in your cmd ( windows ) or terminal ( linux )

```
#import the below module and see what happens
import antigravity
#NOTE - it wont work on online ide
```

Using The Sep Parameter In The Print() Function:
The code provided demonstrates the usage of the print() function to display strings with different separators. The sep parameter of the print() function is utilized to specify the separator between the strings. In the first example, a comma is used as the separator, in the second example, a semicolon is used, and in the third example, an emoji is used.
Time Complexity:
The time complexity of the print() function is $O(n)$, where n represents the total number of characters to be printed. However, specifying a separator has a time complexity of $O(1)$ since it is a constant time operation.
Space Complexity:
The space complexity of the code is also $O(n)$, where n indicates the total number of characters to be printed. This is because the print() function requires memory allocation to store the strings and separators before printing them out.
In summary, the code has a constant time complexity for specifying the separator, and a linear time and space complexity for printing the strings and separators.

```
# using a comma separator
print('apples', 'oranges', 'bananas', sep=', ')
# output: apples, oranges, bananas

# using a semicolon separator
print('one', 'two', 'three', sep=';')
# output: one;two;three

# using an emoji separator
print('????', '????', '????', sep='????')
# output: ????????????????????????
```

Output
apples,
oranges,
bananas
one;two;three
????????????????
????????

## OUTPUT FORMATTING

When it comes to presenting the output of a program, there are multiple approaches available. Data can be displayed in a format that is easily readable by humans, or it can be written to a file for future reference, or even presented in a specific format as required. Oftentimes, users desire greater control over the formatting of the output than simply printing values separated by spaces. To achieve this, there are several techniques and methods available to format the output according to specific requirements.

- To use formatted string literals, begin a string with f or F before the opening quotation mark or triple quotation mark.
- The str. format() method of strings helps a user create a fancier output
- Users can do all the string handling by using string slicing and concatenation operations to create any layout that the users want. The string type has some methods that perform useful operations for padding strings to a given column width.

*Formatting output using String modulo operator(%):*
The % operator in Python can be employed for string formatting. It operates similarly to the printf()-style format in the C language, where the format is specified in the left argument and applied to the right argument. Although Python does not have a printf() function, it encompasses the functionality of the traditional print. To accomplish this, the string class overloads the modulo operator (%), enabling it to perform string formatting. Hence, it is often referred to as the string modulo operator or modulus operator. The string modulo operator (%), which is still available in Python (3.x), continues to be widely used. However, the older style of formatting has been phased out from the language.

```
# Python program showing how to use
# string modulo operator(%) to print
# fancier output

# print integer and float value
print("Geeks : %2d, Portal : %5.2f" % (1, 05.333))

# print integer value
print("Total students : %3d, Boys : %2d" % (240, 120))

# print octal value
print("%7.3o" % (25))

# print exponential value
print("%10.3E" % (356.08977))
```

Output :
Geeks : 1, Portal : 5.33
Total students : 240, Boys : 120
   031
3.561E+02
There are two of those in our example: "%2d" and "%5.2f". The general syntax for

a format placeholder is:
%[flags][width][.precision]type
Let's take a look at the placeholders in our example.

- The first placeholder "%2d" is used for the first component of our tuple, i.e. the integer 1 The number will be printed with 2 characters. As 1 consists only of one digit, the output is padded with 1 leading blank.
- The second one "%5.2f" is a format description for a float number. Like other placeholders, it is introduced with the % character. This is followed by the total number of digits the string should contain. This number includes the decimal point and all the digits, i.e. before and after the decimal point.
- Our float number 05.333 has to be formatted with 5 characters. The decimal part of the number or the precision is set to 2, i.e. the number following the "." in our placeholder. Finally, the last character "f" of our placeholder stands for "float".

**Formatting output using the format method:**
The format() method was introduced in Python 2.6. It offers an alternative approach to string formatting that requires a bit more manual effort. In the format method, users utilize curly braces {} to indicate the positions where variables will be substituted, and they can also provide additional formatting directives. However, it is essential for the user to provide the necessary information for the formatting to take place. This method allows for concatenating elements within an output using positional formatting.
For Example:
Code 1:
Output :

```
# Python program showing
# use of format() method

# using format() method
print('I love {} for "{}!"'.format('micheal', 'micheal'))

# using format() method and referring
# a position of the object
print('{0} and {1}'.format('micheal', 'Portal'))

print('{1} and {0}'.format('micheal', 'Portal'))


# the above formatting can also be done by using f-strings
# Although, this features work only with python 3.6 or above.

print(f"I love {'micheal'} for \"{'micheal'}!\"")

# using format() method and referring
# a position of the object
print(f"{'micheal'} and {'Portal'}")
```

I love micheal for " micheal!"
micheal and Portal
Portal and micheal
I love micheal for "micheal!"

micheal and Portal

The format fields, denoted by the curly braces {}, along with the characters within them, are replaced with the objects that are passed into the format() method. These objects are substituted in the corresponding format fields based on their position. By using a number within the brackets, it is possible to refer to the position of the object passed into the format() method, allowing for precise substitution and formatting.

```python
# Python program showing
# a use of format() method

# combining positional and keyword arguments
print('Number one portal is {0}, {1}, and {other}.'
    .format('micheal', 'For', other ='micheal'))

# using format() method with number
print("micheal :{0:2d}, Portal :{1:8.2f}".
    format(12, 00.546))

# Changing positional argument
print("Second argument: {1:3d}, first one: {0:7.2f}".
    format(47.42, 11))

print("micheal: {a:5d}, Portal: {p:8.2f}".
    format(a = 453, p = 59.058))
```

Code 2:

Output:
Number one portal is micheal, For, and micheal.
Micheal :12, Portal :    0.55
Second argument:  11, first one:   47.42

```python
# Python program to
# show format() is
# used in dictionary

tab = {'micheal': 4127, 'for': 4098, 'micheal': 8637678}

# using format() in dictionary
print('micheal: {0[micheal]:d}; For: {0[for]:d}; '
    'micheal: {0[micheal]:d}'.format(tab))

data = dict(fun ="michealmick", adj ="Portal")

# using format() in dictionary
print("I love {fun} computer {adj}".format(**data))
```

micheal:    453,
Portal:   59.06

Code 3:

Output:
Micheal:    4127;
For:        4098;
micheal:
8637678
I            love
michealmick
computer Portal

Formatting output using the String method :

The presented output is formatted using string slicing and concatenation operations. The string data type offers several methods that aid in achieving more sophisticated output formatting. Some of these methods include str.ljust(), str.rjust(), and str.center(), which facilitate aligning the text to the left, right, or center of a given width, respectively. By utilizing these methods, one can enhance the visual presentation and formatting of the output.

```python
# Python program to
# format a output using
# string() method

cstr = "I love michealmick"

# Printing the center aligned
# string with fillchr
print ("Center aligned string with fillchr: ")
print (cstr.center(40, '#'))

# Printing the left aligned
# string with "-" padding
print ("The left aligned string is : ")
print (cstr.ljust(40, '-'))

# Printing the right aligned string
# with "-" padding
print ("The right aligned string is : ")
print (cstr.rjust(40, '-'))
```

Output:

Center aligned string with fillchr:
###########I love michealmick###########
The left aligned string is :
I love michealmick--------------------
The right aligned string is :
--------------------I love michealmick

## CHAPTER THREE: UNDERSTANDING DATA TYPES

Data types serve as the fundamental classification or categorization of data items, outlining the specific nature of values and the permissible operations that can be executed on each data entity. In Python programming, owing to its object-oriented nature, data types are essentially represented as classes, while variables function as instances or objects derived from these classes. Python encompasses a range of standard or built-in data types, encapsulating the following:

- Numeric
- Sequence Type
- Boolean
- Set
- Dictionary
- Binary Types( memoryview, bytearray, bytes)

## TYPE() FUNCTION?

The type() method is used to declare the values of various data types and to check their data types. Consider the following scenarios.
# DataType Output: str
x = "Hello World"
# DataType Output: int
x = 50
# DataType Output: float
x = 60.5
# DataType Output: complex
x = 3j
# DataType Output: list
x = ["micheal", "for", "micheal"]
# DataType Output: tuple
x = ("micheal", "for", "micheal")
# DataType Output: range
x = range(10)
# DataType Output: dict
x = {"name": "Suraj", "age": 24}
# DataType Output: set
x = {"micheal", "for", "micheal"}
# DataType Output: frozenset
x = frozenset({"micheal", "for", "micheal"})

# DataType Output: bool
x = True
# DataType Output: bytes
x = b"micheal"
# DataType Output: bytearray
x = bytearray(4)
# DataType Output: memoryview
x = memoryview(bytes(6))
# DataType Output: NoneType
x = None

## NUMERIC DATA TYPE IN PYTHON

In Python, the numeric data type represents data with a numeric value. An integer, a floating number, or even a complex number can be used to represent a numeric value. In Python, these values are defined as Python int, Python float, and Python complicated classes.

- Integers – The int class represents this value. It comprises full numbers that are positive or negative (no fractions or decimals). In Python, there is no limit on the length of an integer number.
- Float – The float class represents this value. It is a floating-point representation of a real number. A decimal point is used to specify it. To express scientific notation, the letter e or E followed by a positive or negative number may be inserted.
- Complex Numbers – A complex class represents a complex number. The formula is (real part) + (imaginary part)j. For instance, 2+3j

Note – type() function is used to determine the type of data type.

```
# Python program to
# demonstrate numeric value

a = 5
print("Type of a: ", type(a))

b = 5.0
print("\nType of b: ", type(b))

c = 2 + 4j
print("\nType of c: ", type(c))
```

Output:
Type of a:  <class 'int'>
Type of b:  <class 'float'>
Type of c:  <class 'complex'>

73

## SEQUENCE DATA TYPE IN PYTHON

The arrangement In Python, a data type is an ordered collection of related or dissimilar data types. Sequences enable the structured and efficient storage of several variables. Python has several types:

- Python List
- Python String
- Python Tuple

## STRING DATA TYPE

Strings in Python are byte arrays that represent Unicode characters. A string is a group of one or more characters enclosed in a single, double, or triple quotation. There is no character data type in Python; a character is an one-length string. The str class represents it.

**Creating String**

Strings in Python can be constructed using single, double, or even triple quotes.

```
# Python Program for
# Creation of String
# Creating a String
# with single Quotes
String1 = 'Welcome to the micheal World'
print("String with the use of Single Quotes: ")
print(String1)
# Creating a String
# with double Quotes
String1 = "I'm a micheal"
print("\nString with the use of Double Quotes: ")
print(String1)
print(type(String1))
# Creating a String
# with triple Quotes
String1 = '''I'm a micheal and I live in a world of "micheal"'''
print("\nString with the use of Triple Quotes: ")
print(String1)
print(type(String1))
# Creating String with triple
# Quotes allows multiple lines
String1 = '''micheal
  For
```

Life'''
print("\nCreating a multiline String: ")
print(String1)
Output:
String with the use of Single Quotes:
Welcome to the micheal World
String with the use of Double Quotes:
I'm a micheal
<class 'str'>
String with the use of Triple Quotes:
I'm a micheal and I live in a world of "Geeks"
<class 'str'>
Creating a multiline String:
Micheal
        For
        Life

**Accessing elements of String**

Individual characters of a String can be obtained in Python using the Indexing function. Negative Indexing permits negative address references to access characters from the String's back end, for example, -1 corresponds to the final character, -2 refers to the second last character, and so on.

```
# Python Program to Access
# characters of String

String1 = "michealmick"
print("Initial String: ")
print(String1)

# Printing First character
print("\nFirst character of String is: ")
print(String1[0])

# Printing Last character
print("\nLast character of String is: ")
print(String1[-1])
```

Output:
Initial String:
michealmick
First character of String is:
G
Last character of String is:
S

# LIST DATA TYPE

Lists are an ordered collection of data, similar to arrays in other languages. It is extremely adaptable since the elements in a list do not have to be of the same kind.

## Creating List

In Python, you may make a list by simply putting the sequence inside the square brackets[].

```
# Creating a List
List = []
print("Initial blank List: ")
print(List)

# Creating a List with
# the use of a String
List = ['michealmick']
print("\nList with the use of String: ")
print(List)

# Creating a List with
# the use of multiple values
List = ["micheal", "mick"]
print("\nList containing multiple values: ")
print(List[0])
print(List[2])

# Creating a Multi-Dimensional List
# (By Nesting a list inside a List)
List = [['micheal'], ['Geeks']]
print("\nMulti-Dimensional List: ")
print(List)
```

Output:
Initial blank List:
[]
List with the use of String:
['michealmick']
List containing multiple values:
Micheal
Micheal
Multi-Dimensional List:
[['micheal'], ['mick']]

## Python Access List Items

To retrieve specific elements from a list, the index number is utilized. In Python, the index operator [ ] allows access to individual items within a list. An intriguing feature is the utilization of negative sequence indexes, which denote positions relative to the end of the array. Consequently, instead of calculating the offset, as in the case of List[len(List)-3], simply employing List[-3] suffices. Negative indexing enables counting from the end of the list, with -1 denoting the last item, -2 representing the second-last item, and so forth.

```
# Python program to demonstrate
# accessing of element from list

# Creating a List with
# the use of multiple values
List = ["micheal", "mick"]

# accessing a element from the
# list using index number
print("Accessing element from the list")
print(List[0])
print(List[2])

# accessing a element using
# negative indexing
print("Accessing element using negative indexing")

# print the last element of list
print(List[-1])

# print the third last element of list
print(List[-3])
```

Output:
Accessing element from the list
Micheal
Mick
Accessing element using negative indexing
Micheal
Mick

## Tuple Data Type

A tuple, like a list, is an ordered collection of Python objects. The main distinction between a tuple and a list is that tuples are immutable, which means they cannot be updated once they are generated. A tuple class is used to represent it.

**Creating a Tuple**

Tuples are produced in Python by inserting a sequence of values separated by a 'comma', with or without the use of parenthesis to group the data sequence. Tuples can have any number of elements and any datatype (such as strings, integers, lists, and so on). Tuples can also be formed with a single element, although it is more difficult. A single element in the parentheses is insufficient; a following 'comma' is required to make it a tuple.

```python
# Creating an empty tuple
Tuple1 = ()
print("Initial empty Tuple: ")
print(Tuple1)
# Creating a Tuple with
# the use of Strings
Tuple1 = ('micheal', 'For')
print("\nTuple with the use of String: ")
print(Tuple1)
# Creating a Tuple with
# the use of list
list1 = [1, 2, 4, 5, 6]
print("\nTuple using List: ")
print(tuple(list1))
# Creating a Tuple with the
# use of built-in function
Tuple1 = tuple('micheal')
print("\nTuple with the use of function: ")
print(Tuple1)
# Creating a Tuple
# with nested tuples
Tuple1 = (0, 1, 2, 3)
Tuple2 = ('python', 'micheal')
Tuple3 = (Tuple1, Tuple2)
print("\nTuple with nested tuples: ")
print(Tuple3)
```

Output:

Initial empty Tuple:

()

Tuple with the use of String:

('micheal', 'For')

Tuple using List:

(1, 2, 4, 5, 6, 7, 8)

Tuple with the use of function:

('m', 'i', 'c', 'h', 'e', 'a', 'l')

Tuple with nested tuples:

((0, 1, 2, 3, 4, 5, 6), ('python', 'micheal'))

Note – Tuple packing is the process of creating a Python tuple without using parentheses.

## Access Tuple Items

Refer to the index number to retrieve the tuple elements. To retrieve a tuple item, use the index operator []. The index must be a positive integer. Nested indexing is used to access nested tuples.

```
# Python program to
# demonstrate accessing tuple

tuple1 = tuple([1, 2, 3, 4, 5])

# Accessing element using indexing
print("First element of tuple")
print(tuple1[0])

# Accessing element from last
# negative indexing
print("\nLast element of tuple")
print(tuple1[-1])

print("\nThird last element of tuple")
print(tuple1[-3])
```

Output:
First element of tuple
1
Last element of tuple
5
Third last element of tuple
3

## BOOLEAN DATA TYPE IN PYTHON

True or False are the two built-in values for data types. Boolean objects with the value True is truthy (true), whereas those with the value False are falsy (false). Non-Boolean items, on the other hand, can be evaluated in a Boolean context and judged to be true or false. The class bool represents it. Note: False and True with capital 'T' and 'F' are valid booleans; otherwise, Python will throw an exception.

```
# Python program to
# demonstrate boolean type

print(type(True))
print(type(False))

print(type(true))
```

Output:
<class 'bool'>
<class 'bool'>
Traceback (most recent call last):
 File "/home/7e8862763fb66153d70824
099d4f5fb7.py", line 8, in
   print(type(true))
NameError: name 'true' is not defined

## SET DATA TYPE IN PYTHON

A Set in Python is an unordered collection of data types that is iterable, changeable, and does not contain duplicate entries. The order of the items in a set is unknown, yet it may contain several elements.

**Create a Set in Python**

Sets may be formed by using the built-in set() method with an iterable object or a sequence enclosed in curly braces separated by a 'comma'. A set's elements do not have to be of the same type; other mixed-up data type values can also be provided to the set.

```python
# Python program to demonstrate
# Creation of Set in Python
# Creating a Set
set1 = set()
print("Initial blank Set: ")
print(set1)
# Creating a Set with
# the use of a String
set1 = set("michealmick")
print("\nSet with the use of String: ")
print(set1)
# Creating a Set with
# the use of a List
set1 = set(["micheal", "For", "micheal"])
print("\nSet with the use of List: ")
print(set1)
# Creating a Set with
# a mixed type of values
# (Having numbers and strings)
set1 = set([1, 2, 'micheal', 4, 'For', 6, 'micheal'])
print("\nSet with the use of Mixed Values")
print(set1)
```

Output:
Initial blank Set:
set()
Set with the use of String:
{'F', 'o', 'G', 's', 'r', 'k', 'e'}
Set with the use of List:
{'micheal', 'For'}
Set with the use of Mixed Values
{1, 2, 4, 6, 'micheal', 'For'}

**Access Set Items**

Set items cannot be retrieved using an index because sets are unordered and the elements have no index. However, you may use the in the keyword to loop over the set elements or to inquire if a particular value is present in a set.

```python
# Python program to demonstrate
```

```python
# Accessing of elements in a set
# Creating a set
set1 = set(["micheal", "For", "micheal"])
print("\nInitial set")
print(set1)
# Accessing element using
# for loop
print("\nElements of set: ")
for i in set1:
 print(i, end=" ")
# Checking the element
# using in keyword
print("micheal" in set1)
```
Output:
Initial set:
{'micheal', 'For'}
Elements of set:
micheal For
True

## DICTIONARY DATA TYPE

In Python, a dictionary serves as an unordered assemblage of data values, functioning as a storage mechanism for key-value pairs. Unlike other data types that solely accommodate a single value per element, dictionaries enable the association of a specific key with its corresponding value. The utilization of key-value pairs enhances the efficiency and optimization of dictionaries. Within a dictionary, each key-value pair is segregated by a colon (:), and individual keys are delimited by commas to facilitate differentiation.

**Create a Dictionary**
In Python, a dictionary is generated by enclosing a series of elements within curly braces ({}) and separating them with commas. The elements consist of key-value pairs, where values can be of any data type and can be duplicated. However, keys must be unique and immutable.

Alternatively, the dict() built-in function can be employed to create a dictionary. To generate an empty dictionary, simply enclose curly braces without any elements. It is important to note that dictionary keys are case-sensitive, implying that keys with the same name but varying cases will be treated as distinct entities.
# Creating an empty Dictionary

```
Dict = {}
print("Empty Dictionary: ")
print(Dict)
# Creating a Dictionary
# with Integer Keys
Dict = {1: 'micheal', 2: 'For', 3: 'micheal'}
print("\nDictionary with the use of Integer Keys: ")
print(Dict)
# Creating a Dictionary
# with Mixed keys
Dict = {'Name': 'micheal', 1: [1, 2, 3, 4]}
print("\nDictionary with the use of Mixed Keys: ")
print(Dict)
# Creating a Dictionary
# with dict() method
Dict = dict({1: 'micheal', 2: 'For', 3: 'micheal'})
print("\nDictionary with the use of dict(): ")
print(Dict)
# Creating a Dictionary
# with each item as a Pair
Dict = dict([(1, 'micheal'), (2, 'For')])
print("\nDictionary with each item as a pair: ")
print(Dict)
```
Output:

Empty Dictionary:

{}

Dictionary with the use of Integer Keys:

{1: 'micheal', 2: 'For', 3: ' micheal'}

Dictionary with the use of Mixed Keys:

{1: [1, 2, 3, 4], 'Name': ' micheal'}

Dictionary with the use of dict():

{1: ' micheal', 2: 'For', 3: ' micheal'}

Dictionary with each item as a pair:

{1: ' micheal', 2: 'For'}

**Accessing Key-value in Dictionary**

Refer to the key name of a dictionary to access its elements. Inside square brackets, key can be utilized. There is also a function named get() that may be used to obtain an element from a dictionary.

```python
# Python program to demonstrate
# accessing a element from a Dictionary

# Creating a Dictionary
Dict = {1: 'micheal', 'name': 'For', 3: 'micheal'}

# accessing a element using key
print("Accessing a element using key:")
print(Dict['name'])

# accessing a element using get()
# method
print("Accessing a element using get:")
print(Dict.get(3))
```

Output:
Accessing a element using key:
For
Accessing a element using get:
Micheal

# CHAPTER FOUR: UNDERSTANDING PYTHON STRING

In Python, a string is a data structure that denotes a sequential arrangement of characters. It is classified as an immutable data type, signifying that once a string is created, it cannot be altered. Strings find extensive application across various domains, serving purposes such as storing and manipulating textual data, representing information like names, addresses, and other text-based data formats.
Example:
"michealmick"
Python lacks a character data type; a single character is essentially an one-length string. Square brackets can be used to access string components.
print("A Computer Science portal by michealmick")
Output:
A Computer Science portal by michealmick.

## CREATING A STRING

Strings in Python can be constructed using single, double, or even triple quotes.
# Python Program for
# Creation of String
# Creating a String
# with single Quotes
String1 = 'Welcome to the micheals World'
print("String with the use of Single Quotes: ")
print(String1)
# Creating a String
# with double Quotes
String1 = "I'm a micheals"
print("\nString with the use of Double Quotes: ")
print(String1)
# Creating a String
# with triple Quotes
String1 = '''I'm a mick and I live in a world of "micheal"'''
print("\nString with the use of Triple Quotes: ")
print(String1)
# Creating String with triple
# Quotes allows multiple lines
String1 = '''micheal
    For

Life'''
print("\nCreating a multiline String: ")
print(String1)
Output:
String with the use of Single Quotes:
Welcome to the micheals World
String with the use of Double Quotes:
I'm a micheals
String with the use of Triple Quotes:
I'm a mick and I live in a world of "micheals"
Creating a multiline String:
Micheal
    For
    Life

## ACCESSING CHARACTERS IN PYTHON STRING

In Python, individual characters within a string can be accessed using the indexing technique. Indexing enables both positive and negative address references to retrieve characters from the string. For instance, -1 indicates the last character, -2 denotes the second-to-last character, and so forth. However, attempting to access an index outside the valid range will result in an IndexError. It's important to note that only integers are permitted as valid indices while passing a float or any other incompatible data type will trigger a TypeError.

| M | I | C | H | E | A | L | M | I | C | K |
|---|---|---|---|---|---|---|---|---|---|---|
| 0 | 1 | 2 | 3 | 4 | 5 | 6 | 7 | 8 | 9 | 10 |

| -11 | -10 | -9 | -8 | -7 | -6 | -5 | -4 | -3 | -2 | -1 |
|---|---|---|---|---|---|---|---|---|---|---|

```
# Python Program to Access
# characters of String

String1 = "michealmick"
print("Initial String: ")
print(String1)

# Printing First character
print("\nFirst character of String is: ")
print(String1[0])

# Printing Last character
print("\nLast character of String is: ")
print(String1[-1])
```

Output:
Initial String:
michealmick
First character of String is:
G
Last cha racter of String is:
S


## REVERSING A PYTHON STRING

We may also reverse them using Accessing Characters from a String. Reversing a string is as simple as writing [::-1] and the string will be reversed.

```
#Program to reverse a string
gfg = "michealmick"
print(gfg[::-1])
```

Output:
Michealmick
We can also reverse a string by using built-in join and reversed function.

```
# Program to reverse a string

gfg = "michealmick"

# Reverse the string using reversed and join function
gfg = "".join(reversed(gfg))

print(gfg)
```

Output:
Michealmick

## STRING SLICING

The slicing technique is used to access a range of characters in the String. A Slicing operator (colon) is used to slice a String.

```
# Python Program to
# demonstrate String slicing

# Creating a String
String1 = "michealmick"
print("Initial String: ")
print(String1)

# Printing 3rd to 12th character
print("\nSlicing characters from 3-11: ")
print(String1[3:11])

# Printing characters between
# 3rd and 2nd last character
print("\nSlicing characters between " +
    "3rd and 2nd last character: ")
print(String1[3:-2])
```

Output:
Initial String:
michealmick
Slicing characters from 3-11:
healmick
Slicing characters between 3rd and 2nd last character:
Healmi

## DELETING/UPDATING FROM A STRING

In Python, it is not possible to update or delete individual characters within a string. Such operations will result in errors since item assignment or deletion is not supported for strings. However, the entire string can be

87

deleted using the built-in del keyword. This is due to the immutability of strings, which means that once a string is assigned, its elements cannot be modified. Instead, new strings can be assigned to the same name if desired changes are needed.

Updation of a character:

```
# Python Program to Update
# character of a String
String1 = "Hello, I'm a mick"
print("Initial String: ")
print(String1)
# Updating a character of the String
## As python strings are immutable, they don't support item updation
directly
### there are following two ways
#1
list1 = list(String1)
list1[2] = 'p'
String2 = ''.join(list1)
print("\nUpdating character at 2nd Index: ")
print(String2)
#2
String3 = String1[0:2] + 'p' + String1[3:]
print(String3)
```

Output:
Initial String:
Hello, I'm a mick
Updating character at 2nd Index:
Heplo, I'm a mick
Heplo, I'm a mick
Updating Entire String:

```
# Python Program to Update
# entire String
String1 = "Hello, I'm a mick"
print("Initial String: ")
print(String1)
# Updating a String
String1 = "Welcome to the micheals World"
print("\nUpdated String: ")
print(String1)
```

Output:

Initial String:

Hello, I'm a mick

Updated String:

Welcome to the micheals World

Deletion of a character:

```
# Python Program to Delete
# characters from a String
String1 = "Hello, I'm a mick"
print("Initial String: ")
print(String1)
# Deleting a character
# of the String
String2 = String1[0:2] + String1[3:]
print("\nDeleting character at 2nd Index: ")
print(String2)
```

Output:

Initial String:

Hello, I'm a mick

Deleting character at 2nd Index:

Helo, I'm a mick

**Deleting Entire String:**

The del keyword allows for the deletion of the entire string. Furthermore, attempting to print the string will result in an error since String has been erased and is no longer accessible for printing.

```
# Python Program to Delete
# entire String
String1 = "Hello, I'm a mick"
print("Initial String: ")
print(String1)
# Deleting a String
# with the use of del
del String1
print("\nDeleting entire String: ")
print(String1)
```

Error:

```
Traceback (most recent call last):
File "/home/e4b8f2170f140da99d2fe57d9d8c6a94.py", line 12, in
print(String1)
NameError: name 'String1' is not defined
```

# ESCAPE SEQUENCING IN PYTHON

Printing strings that contain single or double quotes can result in a SyntaxError. This occurs because the string itself already includes single or double quotes, making it challenging to print using either of these quotation marks. To overcome this issue, we have two options: using triple quotes or employing escape sequences. Escape sequences begin with a backslash and have different interpretations. When single quotes are used to represent a string, all single quotes within the string need to be escaped, and the same applies to double quotes.

```
# Python Program for
# Escape Sequencing
# of String
# Initial String
String1 = '''I'm a "mick"'''
print("Initial String with use of Triple Quotes: ")
print(String1)
# Escaping Single Quote
String1 = 'I\'m a "mick"'
print("\nEscaping Single Quote: ")
print(String1)
# Escaping Double Quotes
String1 = "I'm a \"mick\""
print("\nEscaping Double Quotes: ")
print(String1)
# Printing Paths with the
# use of Escape Sequences
String1 = "C:\\Python\\micks\\"
print("\nEscaping Backslashes: ")
print(String1)
# Printing Paths with the
# use of Tab
String1 = "Hi\tmicks"
print("\nTab: ")
print(String1)
# Printing Paths with the
# use of New Line
String1 = "Python\nmicks"
print("\nNew Line: ")
print(String1)
Output:
```

Initial String with use of Triple Quotes:
I'm a "mick"
Escaping Single Quote:
I'm a "mick"
Escaping Double Quotes:
I'm a "mick"
Escaping Backslashes:
C:\Python\micks\
Tab:
Hi   micks

New Line:
Python
micks
To ignore escape sequences within a string, you can use the "r" or "R" prefix. This indicates that the string is a raw string, and any escape sequences within it should be disregarded.

```
# Printing hello in octal
String1 = "\110\145\154\154\157"
print("\nPrinting in Octal with the use of Escape Sequences: ")
print(String1)
# Using raw String to
# ignore Escape Sequences
String1 = r"This is \110\145\154\154\157"
print("\nPrinting Raw String in Octal Format: ")
print(String1)
# Printing micks in HEX
String1 = "This is \x47\x65\x65\x6b\x73 in \x48\x45\x58"
print("\nPrinting in HEX with the use of Escape Sequences: ")
print(String1)
# Using raw String to
# ignore Escape Sequences
String1 = r"This is \x47\x65\x65\x6b\x73 in \x48\x45\x58"
print("\nPrinting Raw String in HEX Format: ")
print(String1)
```

Output:
Printing in Octal with the use of Escape Sequences:
Hello
Printing Raw String in Octal Format:
This is \110\145\154\154\157
Printing in HEX with the use of Escape Sequences:

This is micks in HEX
Printing Raw String in HEX Format:
This is \x47\x65\x65\x6b\x73 in \x48\x45\x58

## FORMATTING OF STRINGS

In Python, strings can be formatted using the format() method, which is a highly flexible and powerful tool. The format() method allows you to specify placeholders using curly braces {} within the string. These placeholders can hold arguments based on their position or be assigned using keywords to determine the desired order of formatting.

```
# Python Program for
# Formatting of Strings
# Default order
String1 = "{} {} {}".format('micks', 'For', 'Life')
print("Print String in default order: ")
print(String1)
# Positional Formatting
String1 = "{1} {0} {2}".format('micks', 'For', 'Life')
print("\nPrint String in Positional order: ")
print(String1)
# Keyword Formatting
String1 = "{l} {f} {g}".format(g='micks', f='For', l='Life')
print("\nPrint String in order of Keywords: ")
print(String1)
```

Output:
Print String in default order:
micks For Life
Print String in Positional order:
For micks Life
Print String in order of Keywords:
Life For micks

Integers, including binary and hexadecimal representations, as well as floats, can be formatted in different ways using format specifiers. This allows you to round them or display them in exponent form based on your requirements.

```
# Formatting of Integers
String1 = "{0:b}".format(16)
print("\nBinary representation of 16 is ")
print(String1)
# Formatting of Floats
```

String1 = "{0:e}".format(165.6458)
print("\nExponent representation of 165.6458 is ")
print(String1)
# Rounding off Integers
String1 = "{0:.2f}".format(1/6)
print("\none-sixth is : ")
print(String1)
Output:
Binary representation of 16 is
10000
Exponent representation of 165.6458 is
1.656458e+02
one-sixth is :
0.17
You can align a string to the left or center using format specifiers, denoted by the left() and center(^) methods respectively. These alignment options are specified by using a colon (:) followed by the desired alignment specifier within the format.
# String alignment
String1 = "|{:<10}|{:^10}|{:>10}|".format('micks',
    'for',
    'micks')
print("\nLeft, center and right alignment with Formatting: ")
print(String1)
# To demonstrate aligning of spaces
String1 = "\n{0:^16} was founded in {1:<4}!".format("micksformicks",
    2009)
print(String1)
Output:
Left, center and right alignment with Formatting:
|micks   |   for    |     micks|
 Micksformicks  was founded in 2009 !
Old style formatting was done without the use of format method by using % operator
# Python Program for
# Old Style Formatting
# of Integers
Integer1 = 12.3456789
print("Formatting in 3.2f format: ")
print('The value of Integer1 is %3.2f' % Integer1)
print("\nFormatting in 3.4f format: ")

print('The value of Integer1 is %3.4f' % Integer1)
Output:
Formatting in 3.2f format:
The value of Integer1 is 12.35
Formatting in 3.4f format:
The value of Integer1 is 12.3457

## PYTHON STRING CONSTANTS

| Built-In Function | Description |
|---|---|
| string.ascii_letters | Concatenation of the ascii_lowercase and ascii_uppercase constants. |
| string.ascii_lowercase | Concatenation of lowercase letters |
| string.ascii_uppercase | Concatenation of uppercase letters |
| string.digits | Digit in strings |
| string.hexdigits | Hexadigit in strings |
| string.letters | concatenation of the strings lowercase and uppercase |
| string.lowercase | A string must contains lowercase letters. |
| string.octdigits | Octadigit in a string |
| string.punctuation | ASCII characters having punctuation characters. |
| string.printable | String of characters which are printable |
| String.endswith() | Returns True if a string ends with the given suffix otherwise returns False |
| String.startswith() | Returns True if a string starts with the given prefix otherwise returns False |
| String.isdigit() | Returns "True" if all characters in the string are digits, Otherwise, It returns "False". |
| String.isalpha() | Returns "True" if all characters in the string are |

| | |
|---|---|
| | alphabets, Otherwise, It returns "False". |
| string.isdecimal() | Returns true if all characters in a string are decimal. |
| str.format() | one of the string formatting methods in Python3, which allows multiple substitutions and value formatting. |
| String.index | Returns the position of the first occurrence of substring in a string |
| string.uppercase | A string must contain uppercase letters. |
| string.whitespace | A string containing all characters that are considered whitespace. |
| string.swapcase() | Method converts all uppercase characters to lowercase and vice versa of the given string, and returns it |

## DEPRECATED STRING FUNCTIONS

| Built-In Function | Description |
|---|---|
| string.Isdecimal | Returns true if all characters in a string are decimal |
| String.Isalnum | Returns true if all the characters in a given string are alphanumeric. |
| string.Istitle | Returns True if the string is a title cased string |
| String.partition | splits the string at the first occurrence of the separator and returns a tuple. |
| String.Isidentifier | Check whether a string is a valid identifier or not. |
| String.len | Returns the length of the string. |
| String.rindex | Returns the highest index of |

| | the substring inside the string if substring is found. |
|---|---|
| String.Max | Returns the highest alphabetical character in a string. |
| String.min | Returns the minimum alphabetical character in a string. |
| String.splitlines | Returns a list of lines in the string. |
| string.capitalize | Return a word with its first character capitalized. |
| string.expandtabs | Expand tabs in a string replacing them by one or more spaces |
| string.find | Return the lowest indexing a sub string. |
| string.rfind | find the highest index. |
| string.count | Return the number of (non-overlapping) occurrences of substring sub in string |
| string.lower | Return a copy of s, but with upper case, letters converted to lower case. |
| string.split | Return a list of the words of the string, If the optional second argument sep is absent or None |
| string.rsplit() | Return a list of the words of the string s, scanning s from the end. |
| rpartition() | Method splits the given string into three parts |
| string.splitfields | Return a list of the words of the string when only used with two arguments. |
| string.join | Concatenate a list or tuple of words with intervening occurrences of sep. |
| string.strip() | It returns a copy of the string |

| | |
|---|---|
| | with both leading and trailing white spaces removed |
| string.lstrip | Return a copy of the string with leading white spaces removed. |
| string.rstrip | Return a copy of the string with trailing white spaces removed. |
| string.swapcase | Converts lower case letters to upper case and vice versa. |
| string.translate | Translate the characters using table |
| string.upper | lower case letters converted to upper case. |
| string.ljust | left-justify in a field of given width. |
| string.rjust | Right-justify in a field of given width. |
| string.center() | Center-justify in a field of given width. |
| string-zfill | Pad a numeric string on the left with zero digits until the given width is reached. |
| string.replace | Return a copy of string s with all occurrences of substring old replaced by new. |
| string.casefold() | Returns the string in lowercase which can be used for caseless comparisons. |
| string.encode | Encodes the string into any encoding supported by Python. The default encoding is utf-8. |
| string.maketrans | Returns a translation table usable for str.translate() |

## ADVANTAGES OF STRING

Strings have extensive use in various operations, serving as a fundamental data type for storing and manipulating textual information. They are employed for representing names, addresses, and other forms of data that can be expressed as text.

Python offers a wide range of string methods, providing flexibility in manipulating and working with strings. These methods simplify common tasks like converting strings to uppercase or lowercase, replacing substrings, and splitting strings into lists.

It is important to note that strings in Python are immutable, meaning that once created, they cannot be changed. This immutability can be advantageous as it ensures the string's value remains constant and predictable.

Python natively supports strings, eliminating the need to import additional libraries or modules for string operations. This simplicity allows for easy integration and reduces code complexity. Moreover, Python's concise syntax facilitates the creation and manipulation of strings, resulting in code that is both readable and efficient.

Drawbacks of String

When working with large text data, strings can become inefficient due to their limitations. For instance, when extensive operations are required, such as replacing substrings or splitting the string into multiple substrings, it can lead to slow execution and high resource consumption.

Strings can also pose challenges when representing complex data structures like lists or dictionaries. In such cases, using alternative data types such as lists or dictionaries proves to be more efficient. These data types provide better flexibility and easier manipulation of the data.

# CHAPTER FIVE: UNDERSTANDING PYTHON LISTS

Python lists serve as dynamic arrays, similar to that declared in other programming languages such as vectors in C++ or ArrayLists in Java. In simpler terms, a list is a collection of items enclosed within square brackets [ ] and separated by commas. It is a sequence data type designed to store a collection of data elements. Tuples and strings are also examples of sequence data types.

Example of list in Python

Here we are creating Python List using [].

```
Var = ["micks", "for", "micks"]
print(Var)
```

Output:

```
["micks", "for", "micks"]
```

Lists are fundamental containers in Python and are an essential part of the language. One of the key advantages of lists is their ability to accommodate different types of data, making them a versatile tool in Python. A list can consist of various data types, including integers, strings, and objects. This flexibility makes lists a powerful feature in Python.

## CREATING A LIST IN PYTHON

In Python, lists can be created simply by enclosing a sequence of elements within square brackets []. Unlike sets, lists do not require a built-in function for their creation. You can directly define a list by placing the desired elements inside the brackets.

Example 1: Creating a list in Python

```
# Python program to demonstrate
# Creation of List
# Creating a List
List = []
print("Blank List: ")
print(List)
# Creating a List of numbers
List = [10, 20, 14]
print("\nList of numbers: ")
print(List)
# Creating a List of strings and accessing
# using index
List = ["micks", "For", "micks"]
print("\nList Items: ")
```

```
print(List[0])
print(List[2])
```
Output
Blank List:
[]
List of numbers:
[10, 20, 14]
List Items:
Geeks
Geeks
Complexities for Creating Lists
Time Complexity: O(1)
Space Complexity: O(n)
Example 2: Creating a list with multiple distinct or duplicate elements
During the creation of a list, it is possible for duplicate values to be
included, each occupying a unique position. This allows for the presence of
multiple distinct or repeated values within the sequence used to construct
the list.

```
# Creating a List with
# the use of Numbers
# (Having duplicate values)
List = [1, 2, 4, 4, 3, 3, 3, 6, 5]
print("\nList with the use of Numbers: ")
print(List)
# Creating a List with
# mixed type of values
# (Having numbers and strings)
List = [1, 2, 'micks', 4, 'For', 6, 'micks']
print("\nList with the use of Mixed Values: ")
print(List)
```
Output
List with the use of Numbers:
[1, 2, 4, 4, 3, 3, 3, 6, 5]
List with the use of Mixed Values:
[1, 2, 'micks', 4, 'For', 6, 'micks']

## ACCESSING ELEMENTS FROM THE LIST

To retrieve specific elements from a list, you can utilize the index operator,
denoted by the square brackets [ ]. The index provided must be an integer,

indicating the position of the desired item within the list. If the list contains nested lists, you can access their elements using nested indexing.

Example 1: Accessing elements from list

```
# Python program to demonstrate
# accessing of element from list
# Creating a List with
# the use of multiple values
List = ["micks", "For", "micks"]
# accessing an element from the
# list using index number
print("Accessing a element from the list")
print(List[0])
print(List[2])
```

Output

Accessing an element from the list
Micks
micks

Example 2: Accessing elements from a multi-dimensional list

```
# Creating a Multi-Dimensional List
# (By Nesting a list inside a List)
List = [['mick', 'For'], ['mick']]
# accessing an element from the
# Multi-Dimensional List using
# index number
print("Accessing a element from a Multi-Dimensional list")
print(List[0][1])
print(List[1][0])
```

Output

Accessing an element from a Multi-Dimensional list
For
Mick

## *NEGATIVE INDEXING*

In Python, negative sequence indexes are used to reference positions from the end of an array. Instead of calculating the offset manually, such as List[len(List)-3], you can simply use List[-3]. Negative indexing allows you to start from the end of the list, where -1 represents the last item, -2 refers to the second-to-last item, and so on.

List = [1, 2, 'mick', 4, 'For', 6, 'mick']

# accessing an element using
# negative indexing
print("Accessing element using negative indexing")
# print the last element of list
print(List[-1])
# print the third last element of list
print(List[-3])
Output
Accessing element using negative indexing
micks
For
Complexities for Accessing elements in a Lists:
Time Complexity: O(1)
Space Complexity: O(1)

## GETTING THE SIZE OF THE PYTHON LIST

Python's len() function is used to determine the length of a list.

```
# Creating a List
List1 = []
print(len(List1))

# Creating a List of numbers
List2 = [10, 20, 14]
print(len(List2))
```

Output
0
3
Taking Input from a Python List
We may accept a list of elements as input like string, integer, float, and so on. However, the default is a string.
Example 1:
# Python program to take space
# separated input as a string
# split and store it to a list
# and print the string list
# input the list as string
string = input("Enter elements (Space-Separated): ")
# split the strings and store it to a list
lst = string.split()
print('The list is:', lst) # printing the list

Output:
Enter elements: michealmick
The list is: ['micheal', 'mick']
Example 2:
```
# input size of the list
n = int(input("Enter the size of list : "))
# store integers in a list using map,
# split and strip functions
lst = list(map(int, input("Enter the integer\
elements:").strip().split()))[:n]
# printing the list
print('The list is:', lst)
```
Output:
Enter the size of list : 4
Enter the integer elements: 6 3 9 10
The list is: [6, 3, 9, 10]

## ADDING ELEMENTS TO A PYTHON LIST

Method 1: Using append() method
To add elements to a list in Python, the built-in append() function is employed. Using append(), you can add one element at a time to the list. If you wish to add multiple elements, you would need to utilize loops in conjunction with the append() method. It is also possible to add tuples to a list using the append() method since tuples are immutable. In contrast to sets, lists can be appended to an existing list by utilizing the append() method.
```
# Python program to demonstrate
# Addition of elements in a List
# Creating a List
List = []
print("Initial blank List: ")
print(List)
# Addition of Elements
# in the List
List.append(1)
List.append(2)
List.append(4)
print("\nList after Addition of Three elements: ")
print(List)
# Adding elements to the List
```

```python
# using Iterator
for i in range(1, 4):
 List.append(i)
print("\nList after Addition of elements from 1-3: ")
print(List)
# Adding Tuples to the List
List.append((5, 6))
print("\nList after Addition of a Tuple: ")
print(List)
# Addition of List to a List
List2 = ['For', 'micks']
List.append(List2)
print("\nList after Addition of a List: ")
print(List)
```
Output
Initial blank List:
[]
List after Addition of Three elements:
[1, 2, 4]
List after Addition of elements from 1-3:
[1, 2, 4, 1, 2, 3]
List after Addition of a Tuple:
[1, 2, 4, 1, 2, 3, (5, 6)]
List after Addition of a List:
[1, 2, 4, 1, 2, 3, (5, 6), ['For', 'micks']]
Complexities for Adding elements in a Lists(append() method):
Time Complexity: O(1)
Space Complexity: O(1)
Method 2: Using insert() method
The append() technique only works for adding entries at the end of a List; insert() is used for adding elements at the proper place. Unlike add(), which requires only one parameter, insert() requires two (position, value).

```python
# Python program to demonstrate
# Addition of elements in a List
# Creating a List
List = [1,2,3,4]
print("Initial List: ")
print(List)
# Addition of Element at
# specific Position
# (using Insert Method)
```

```
List.insert(3, 12)
List.insert(0, 'micks')
print("\nList after performing Insert Operation: ")
print(List)
```
Output
Initial List:
[1, 2, 3, 4]
List after performing Insert Operation:
['micks', 1, 2, 3, 12, 4]
Complexities for Adding elements in a Lists(insert() method):
Time Complexity: O(n)
Space Complexity: O(1)
Method 3: Using extend() method
Aside from the append() and insert() methods, there is one additional technique for adding elements, extend(). This function is used to add several entries to the end of the list at the same time.

```
# Python program to demonstrate
# Addition of elements in a List
# Creating a List
List = [1, 2, 3, 4]
print("Initial List: ")
print(List)

# Addition of multiple elements
# to the List at the end
# (using Extend Method)
List.extend([8, 'micks', 'Always'])
print("\nList after performing Extend Operation: ")
print(List)
```
Output
Initial List:
[1, 2, 3, 4]
List after performing Extend Operation:
[1, 2, 3, 4, 8, 'micks', 'Always']
Complexities for Adding elements in a Lists(extend() method):
Time Complexity: O(n)
Space Complexity: O(1)

## REVERSING A LIST

Python's reverse() function may be used to reverse a list.
# Reversing a list
mylist = [1, 2, 3, 4, 5, 'mick', 'Python']
mylist.reverse()
print(mylist)
Output
['Python', 'mick', 5, 4, 3, 2, 1]

## REMOVING ELEMENTS FROM THE LIST

Method 1: Using remove() method
Elements in the List can be deleted using the built-in remove() method, however an Error occurs if the element does not exist in the list. The Remove() function only removes one element at a time; the iterator is used to remove a range of elements. The item supplied by the delete() function is removed.

Please keep in mind that the delete function in List will only delete the first occurrence of the searched element.

```
# Python program to demonstrate
# Removal of elements in a List
# Creating a List
List = [1, 2, 3, 4, 5, 6,
   7, 8, 9, 10, 11, 12]
print("Initial List: ")
print(List)
# Removing elements from List
# using Remove() method
List.remove(5)
List.remove(6)
print("\nList after Removal of two elements: ")
print(List)
```
Output
Initial List:
[1, 2, 3, 4, 5, 6, 7, 8, 9, 10, 11, 12]
List after Removal of two elements:
[1, 2, 3, 4, 7, 8, 9, 10, 11, 12]
Example 2:
# Creating a List
List = [1, 2, 3, 4, 5, 6,

7, 8, 9, 10, 11, 12]
# Removing elements from List
# using iterator method
for i in range(1, 5):
 List.remove(i)
print("\nList after Removing a range of elements: ")
print(List)
Output
List after Removing a range of elements:
[5, 6, 7, 8, 9, 10, 11, 12]
Complexities for Deleting elements in a Lists(remove() method):
Time Complexity: O(n)
Space Complexity: O(1)
Method 2: Using pop() method
The pop() function may also be used to remove and return an element from a list; however, by default, it only removes the final element of the list; to remove an element from a specified place in the list, the index of the element is supplied as an argument to the pop() method.
List = [1, 2, 3, 4, 5]
# Removing element from the
# Set using the pop() method
List.pop()
print("\nList after popping an element: ")
print(List)
# Removing element at a
# specific location from the
# Set using the pop() method
List.pop(2)
print("\nList after popping a specific element: ")
print(List)
Output
List after popping an element:
[1, 2, 3, 4]
List after popping a specific element:
[1, 2, 4]
Complexities for Deleting elements in a Lists(pop() method):
Time Complexity: O(1)/O(n) (O(1) for removing the last element, O(n) for removing the first and middle elements)
Space Complexity: O(1)

## SLICING OF A LIST

A slice can be used to obtain substrings and sublists. There are several ways to print the entire list with all of its items in Python List, however we utilize the Slice operation to display a selected range of elements from the list. A colon (:) is used to execute the slice operation on Lists.
To print elements from beginning to a range use:
[: Index]
To print elements from end-use:
[:-Index]
To print elements from a specific Index till the end use
[Index:]
To print the whole list in reverse order, use
[::-1]
Note – To print elements of List from rear-end, use Negative Indexes.

| M | I | C | H | E | A | L | M | I | C | K |
|---|---|---|---|---|---|---|---|---|---|---|
| 0 | 1 | 2 | 3 | 4 | 5 | 6 | 7 | 8 | 9 | 10 |
| -11 | -10 | -9 | -8 | -7 | -6 | -5 | -4 | -3 | -2 | -1 |

## UNDERSTANDING SLICING OF LISTS:

pr[0] accesses the first item, 2.
pr[-4] accesses the fourth item from the end, 5.
pr[2:] accesses [5, 7, 11, 13], a list of items from third to last.
pr[:4] accesses [2, 3, 5, 7], a list of items from first to fourth.
pr[2:4] accesses [5, 7], a list of items from third to fifth.
pr[1::2] accesses [3, 7, 13], alternate items, starting from the second item.
# Python program to demonstrate
# Removal of elements in a List
# Creating a List
List = ['M', 'I', 'C', 'H', 'E', 'A',
 'L', 'M', 'I', 'C', 'K', 'S']
print("Initial List: ")
print(List)
# Print elements of a range
# using Slice operation
Sliced_List = List[3:8]

```
print("\nSlicing elements in a range 3-8: ")
print(Sliced_List)
# Print elements from a
# pre-defined point to end
Sliced_List = List[5:]
print("\nElements sliced from 5th "
 "element till the end: ")
print(Sliced_List)
# Printing elements from
# beginning till end
Sliced_List = List[:]
print("\nPrinting all elements using slice operation: ")
print(Sliced_List)
```

Output
Initial List:
['M', 'T', 'C', 'H', 'E', 'A', 'L', 'M', 'T', 'C', 'K', 'S']
Slicing elements in a range 3-8:
['H', 'E', 'A', 'L', 'M']
Elements sliced from 5th element till the end:
['E', 'A', 'L', 'M', 'T', 'C', 'K', 'S']
Printing all elements using slice operation:
['M', 'T', 'C', 'H', 'E', 'A', 'L', 'M', 'T', 'C', 'K', 'S']

## *NEGATIVE INDEX LIST SLICING*

```
# Creating a List
List = ['M', 'T', 'C', 'H', 'E', 'A',
 'L', 'M', 'T', 'C', 'K', 'S']
print("Initial List: ")
print(List)
# Print elements from beginning
# to a pre-defined point using Slice
Sliced_List = List[:-6]
print("\nElements sliced till 6th element from last: ")
print(Sliced_List)
# Print elements of a range
# using negative index List slicing
Sliced_List = List[-6:-1]
print("\nElements sliced from index -6 to -1")
print(Sliced_List)
```

# Printing elements in reverse
# using Slice operation
Sliced_List = List[::-1]
print("\nPrinting List in reverse: ")
print(Sliced_List)
Output
Initial List:
['M', 'T', 'C', 'H', 'E', 'A', 'L', 'M', 'T', 'C', 'K', 'S']
Elements sliced till 6th element from last:
['M', 'T', 'C', 'H', 'E', 'A',]
Elements sliced from index -6 to -1
['M', 'T', 'C', 'K',]
Printing List in reverse:
['S', 'K', 'C', 'T', 'M', 'L', 'A', 'E', 'H', 'C', 'T', 'M']

## LIST COMPREHENSION

In Python, list comprehensions serve the purpose of generating new lists from other iterable objects such as tuples, strings, arrays, and existing lists. A list comprehension is formed by enclosing an expression within brackets, which is then executed for each element, in combination with a for loop that iterates over each element.
Syntax:
newList = [ expression(element) for element in oldList if condition ]
Example:
# Python program to demonstrate list
# comprehension in Python
# below list contains square of all
# odd numbers from range 1 to 10
odd_square = [x ** 2 for x in range(1, 11) if x % 2 == 1]
print(odd_square)
Output
[1, 9, 25, 49, 81]
For better understanding, the above code is similar to as follows:
# for understanding, above generation is same as,
odd_square = []
for x in range(1, 11):
 if x % 2 == 1:
  odd_square.append(x**2)
print(odd_square)
Output

[1, 9, 25, 49, 81]

## LIST METHODS

Python List Methodshas several ways for working with Python lists. We've detailed all of the methods you may use with Python lists below, including append(), copy(), insert(), and others.

| Function | Description |
|---|---|
| Append() | Add an element to the end of the list |
| Extend() | Add all elements of a list to another list |
| Insert() | Insert an item at the defined index |
| Remove() | Removes an item from the list |
| Clear() | Removes all items from the list |
| Index() | Returns the index of the first matched item |
| Count() | Returns the count of the number of items passed as an argument |
| Sort() | Sort items in a list in ascending order |
| Reverse() | Reverse the order of items in the list |
| copy() | Returns a copy of the list |
| min() | Calculates the minimum of all the elements of the List |
| max() | Calculates the maximum of all the elements of the List |
| pop() | Removes and returns the last value from the List or the given index value. |

## ADDING ELEMENT IN LIST

Python append()
Appends and adds elements to the List. In Python, it is used to append elements to the final place of a List.
Syntax: list.append (element)
# Adds List Element as value of List.

111

List = ['Mathematics', 'chemistry', 1997, 2000]
List.append(20544)
print(List)
Output:
['Mathematics', 'chemistry', 1997, 2000, 20544]
Python insert()
Inserts an element at the specified position.
Syntax:
list.insert(<position, element)
Note: The position mentioned should be within the range of List, as in this case between 0 and 4, else wise would throw IndexError.
List = ['Mathematics', 'chemistry', 1997, 2000]
# Insert at index 2 value 10087
List.insert(2, 10087)
print(List)
Output:
['Mathematics', 'chemistry', 10087, 1997, 2000, 20544]
Python extend()
Adds contents to List2 to the end of List1.
Syntax: List1.extend(List2)
List1 = [1, 2, 3]
List2 = [2, 3, 4, 5]
# Add List2 to List1
List1.extend(List2)
print(List1)
# Add List1 to List2 now
List2.extend(List1)
print(List2)
Output:
[1, 2, 3, 2, 3, 4, 5]
[2, 3, 4, 5, 1, 2, 3, 2, 3, 4, 5]

**IMPORTANT FUNCTIONS OF THE PYTHON LIST**

Some important Python List Functions and how to utilize them in a List.
**Python sum()**
Calculates the sum of all the elements of the List.
Syntax: sum(List)
List = [1, 2, 3, 4, 5]
print(sum(List))
Output:

112

15

What if a numerical value is not utilized as a parameter?
The total is only calculated for Numeric numbers; otherwise, a TypeError is thrown.
See example:

```
List = ['gfg', 'abc', 3]
print(sum(List))
```

Output:

```
Traceback (most recent call last):
  File "", line 1, in
    sum(List)
TypeError: unsupported operand type(s) for +: 'int' and 'str'
```

Python count()
Calculates the total number of occurrences of a specified List element.
Syntax: List.count(element)

```
List = [1, 2, 3, 1, 2, 1, 2, 3, 2, 1]
print(List.count(1))
```

Output:

```
4
```

Python length
The overall length of the List is calculated.
Syntax: len(list_name)

```
List = [1, 2, 3, 1, 2, 1, 2, 3, 2, 1]
print(len(List))
```

Output:

```
10
```

Python index()
The index of the first occurrence is returned. The start and finish indices are optional parameters.
Syntax: List.index(element[,start[,end]])

```
List = [1, 2, 3, 1, 2, 1, 2, 3, 2, 1]
print(List.index(2))
```

Output:

```
1
```

Another example:

```
List = [1, 2, 3, 1, 2, 1, 2, 3, 2, 1]
print(List.index(2, 2))
```

Output:

```
4
```

Python min()
Calculates minimum of all the elements of List.

Syntax: min(iterable, *iterables[, key])
numbers = [5, 2, 8, 1, 9]
print(min(numbers))
Output
1
Python max()
Calculates the maximum of all the elements of the List.
Syntax: max(iterable, *iterables[, key])
numbers = [5, 2, 8, 1, 9]
print(max(numbers))
Output
9

### SORT() AND REVERSE() FUNCTIONS

**Python reverse()**
In ascending order, sort the specified data structure (both tuple and list).
The parameters key and reverse_flag are optional, and reverse_flag is set to
False if nothing is supplied via sorted().
Syntax
sorted([list[,key[,Reverse_Flag]]])
 list.sort([key,[Reverse_flag]])
List = [2.3, 4.445, 3, 5.33, 1.054, 2.5]
#Reverse flag is set True
List.sort(reverse=True)
#List.sort().reverse(), reverses the sorted list
print(List)
Output:
[5.33, 4.445, 3, 2.5, 2.3, 1.054]

## DELETION OF LIST ELEMENTS

Many built-in methods, such as pop() and remove(), as well as keywords
such as del, can be used to delete one or more elements, i.e. remove an
element.
Python pop()
The index is not required; if not specified, the last index is used.
list.pop([index]) is the syntax.
IndexErrors occur if the index is not inside the range of the List.
List = [2.3, 4.445, 3, 5.33, 1.054, 2.5]
print(List.pop())
Output:

2.5
List = [2.3, 4.445, 3, 5.33, 1.054, 2.5]
print(List.pop(0))
Output:
2.3
Python del()
The element to be removed is identified by the list name and index.
Syntax: del list.[index]
List = [2.3, 4.445, 3, 5.33, 1.054, 2.5]
del List[0]
print(List)
Output:
[4.445, 3, 5.33, 1.054, 2.5]
Python remove()
The list name and element are used to identify the element to be eliminated.
Syntax: list.remove(element)
List = [2.3, 4.445, 3, 5.33, 1.054, 2.5]
List.remove(3)
print(List)
Output:
[2.3, 4.445, 5.33, 1.054, 2.5]

## BUILT-IN FUNCTIONS WITH LIST

| Function | Description |
|----------|-------------|
| reduce() | apply a particular function passed in its argument to all of the list elements stores the intermediate result and only returns the final summation value |
| sum() | Sums up the numbers in the list |
| ord() | Returns an integer representing the Unicode code point of the given Unicode character |
| cmp() | This function returns 1 if the first list is "greater" than the second list |
| max() | return maximum element of a given list |
| min() | return minimum element of a |

| | given list |
|---|---|
| all() | Returns true if all element is true or if the list is empty |
| any() | return true if any element of the list is true. if the list is empty, return false |
| len() | Returns length of the list or size of the list |
| enumerate() | Returns enumerate object of the list |
| accumulate() | apply a particular function passed in its argument to all of the list elements returns a list containing the intermediate results |
| filter() | tests if each element of a list is true or not |
| map() | returns a list of the results after applying the given function to each item of a given iterable |
| lambda() | This function can have any number of arguments but only one expression, which is evaluated and returned. |

## LIST COMPREHENSION AND SLICING

In Python, list comprehension is an elegant technique to define and generate a list. Lists, like mathematical assertions, can be created in a single line. The syntax of list comprehension is simpler to understand. A list comprehension often consists of the following components:

- Output expression,
- Input sequence,
- A variable representing a member of the input sequence and
- An optional predicate part.

For example :
lst = [x ** 2 for x in range (1, 11) if x % 2 == 1]
here, x ** 2 is output expression,
    range (1, 11) is input sequence,

x is variable and

if x % 2 == 1 is predicate part.

Another example :

lst=[x**2 if x%2==1 else x*2 for x in range(1,11)]

Example 1:

```
# Python program to demonstrate list comprehension in Python
# below list contains square of all odd numbers from
# range 1 to 10
odd_square = [x ** 2 for x in range(1, 11) if x % 2 == 1]
print (odd_square)
# for understanding, above generation is same as,
odd_square = []
for x in range(1, 11):
 if x % 2 == 1:
  odd_square.append(x**2)
print (odd_square)
# below list contains power of 2 from 1 to 8
power_of_2 = [2 ** x for x in range(1, 9)]
print (power_of_2)
#range 1 to 10
lst=[x**2 if x%2==1 else x*2 for x in range(1,11)]
print(lst)
#for understanding ,above "lst" is same as below "lst1"
lst1=[]
for x in range(1,11):
if x%2==1:
 lst1.append(x**2)
else:
 lst1.append(x*2)
print(lst1)
# below list contains prime and non-prime in range 1 to 50
noprimes = [j for i in range(2, 8) for j in range(i*2, 50, i)]
primes = [x for x in range(2, 50) if x not in noprimes]
print (primes)
# list for lowering the characters
print ([x.lower() for x in ["A","B","C"]] )
# list which extracts number
string = "my phone number is : 11122 !!"
print("\nExtracted digits")
numbers = [x for x in string if x.isdigit()]
print (numbers)
```

```
# A list of list for multiplication table
a = 5
table = [[a, b, a * b] for b in range(1, 11)]
print("\nMultiplication Table")
for i in table:
 print (i)
```
Output:
[1, 9, 25, 49, 81]
[1, 9, 25, 49, 81]
[2, 4, 8, 16, 32, 64, 128, 256]
[2, 3, 5, 7, 11, 13, 17, 19, 23, 29, 31, 37, 41, 43, 47]
['a', 'b', 'c']
Extracted digits
['1', '1', '1', '2', '2']
Multiplication Table
[5, 1, 5]
[5, 2, 10]
[5, 3, 15]
[5, 4, 20]
[5, 5, 25]
[5, 6, 30]
[5, 7, 35]
[5, 8, 40]
[5, 9, 45]
[5, 10, 50]

We can retrieve a subset of the list using Python's slicing operator, which has the following syntax:

[start : stop : steps]

which means that slicing will start from index start
will go up to stop in step of steps.
Default value of start is 0, stop is last index of list
and for step it is 1

So [: stop] will slice the list from the beginning to the end index, whereas [start:] would slice the list from the beginning to the end index. Negative steps values indicate right to left traversal rather than left to right traversal, which is why [:: -1] publishes the list in reverse order.

Example 2:

```
# Let us first create a list to demonstrate slicing
# lst contains all number from 1 to 10
lst =list(range(1, 11))
print (lst)
```

```python
# below list has numbers from 2 to 5
lst1_5 = lst[1 : 5]
print (lst1_5)
# below list has numbers from 6 to 8
lst5_8 = lst[5 : 8]
print (lst5_8)
# below list has numbers from 2 to 10
lst1_ = lst[1 : ]
print (lst1_)
# below list has numbers from 1 to 5
lst_5 = lst[: 5]
print (lst_5)
# below list has numbers from 2 to 8 in step 2
lst1_8_2 = lst[1 : 8 : 2]
print (lst1_8_2)
# below list has numbers from 10 to 1
lst_rev = lst[ : : -1]
print (lst_rev)
# below list has numbers from 10 to 6 in step 2
lst_rev_9_5_2 = lst[9 : 4 : -2]
print (lst_rev_9_5_2)
```
Output:
[1, 2, 3, 4, 5, 6, 7, 8, 9, 10]
[2, 3, 4, 5]
[6, 7, 8]
[2, 3, 4, 5, 6, 7, 8, 9, 10]
[1, 2, 3, 4, 5]
[2, 4, 6, 8]
[10, 9, 8, 7, 6, 5, 4, 3, 2, 1]
[10, 8, 6]

The filter function may be used to filter a list depending on some condition specified as a lambda expression as the first parameter and a list as the second argument, as demonstrated below:

Example 3:
```python
import functools
# filtering odd numbers
lst = filter(lambda x : x % 2 == 1, range(1, 20))
print (list(lst))
# filtering odd square which are divisible by 5
lst = filter(lambda x : x % 5 == 0,
  [x ** 2 for x in range(1, 11) if x % 2 == 1])
```

```
print (list(lst))
# filtering negative numbers
lst = filter((lambda x: x < 0), range(-5,5))
print (list(lst))
# implementing max() function, using
print (functools.reduce(lambda a,b: a if (a > b) else b, [7, 12, 45, 100, 15]))
Output:
[1, 3, 5, 7, 9, 11, 13, 15, 17, 19]
[25]
[-5, -4, -3, -2, -1]
100
```

# CHAPTER SIX: UNDERSTANDING PYTHON TUPLES

Tuple is a list-like collection of Python objects. Tuple stores succession of values of any kind, which are indexed by integers. The values of a tuple are separated by 'commas'. Although not required, it is more usual to define a tuple by enclosing the value sequence in parenthesis. This makes it easier to grasp Python tuples.

## CREATING A TUPLE

Tuples is produced in Python by putting a sequence of values separated by a 'comma' with or without the use of parenthesis to group the data sequence.

Tuple packing is the process of creating a Python tuple without using parentheses.

Python application that shows how to add items in a Tuple.

```
# Creating an empty Tuple
Tuple1 = ()
print("Initial empty Tuple: ")
print(Tuple1)
# Creating a Tuple
# with the use of string
Tuple1 = ('micks', 'For')
print("\nTuple with the use of String: ")
print(Tuple1)
# Creating a Tuple with
# the use of list
list1 = [1, 2, 4, 5, 6]
print("\nTuple using List: ")
print(tuple(list1))
# Creating a Tuple
# with the use of built-in function
Tuple1 = tuple('micks')
print("\nTuple with the use of function: ")
print(Tuple1)
```

Output:

Initial empty Tuple:

()

Tuple with the use of String:

('micks', 'For')

Tuple using List:

(1, 2, 4, 5, 6)
Tuple with the use of function:
('M', 'i', 'c', 'k', 's')
Creating a Tuple with Mixed Datatypes.

Tuples can has any number of elements and any datatype (such as strings, integers, lists, and so on). Tuples can also be made from a single element, although it is more difficult. A single element in the parentheses is insufficient; a following 'comma' is required to make it a tuple.

```
# Creating a Tuple
# with Mixed Datatype
Tuple1 = (5, 'Welcome', 7, 'micks')
print("\nTuple with Mixed Datatypes: ")
print(Tuple1)
# Creating a Tuple
# with nested tuples
Tuple1 = (0, 1, 2, 3)
Tuple2 = ('python', 'mick')
Tuple3 = (Tuple1, Tuple2)
print("\nTuple with nested tuples: ")
print(Tuple3)
# Creating a Tuple
# with repetition
Tuple1 = ('micks',) * 3
print("\nTuple with repetition: ")
print(Tuple1)
# Creating a Tuple
# with the use of loop
Tuple1 = ('micks')
n = 5
print("\nTuple with a loop")
for i in range(int(n)):
    Tuple1 = (Tuple1,)
    print(Tuple1)
```

Output:
Tuple with Mixed Datatypes:
(5, 'Welcome', 7, 'Geeks')
Tuple with nested tuples:
((0, 1, 2, 3), ('python', 'geek'))
Tuple with repetition:
('Geeks', 'Geeks', 'Geeks')
Tuple with a loop

('Geeks',)
(('Geeks',),)
((('Geeks',),),)
(((('Geeks',),),),)
((((('Geeks',),),),),)

Complexities for creating tuples:
Time complexity: O(1)
Auxiliary Space : O(n)

## ACCESSING OF TUPLES

Tuples are immutable and often include a series of heterogeneous items that may be retrieved by unpacking or indexing (or, in the case of named tuples, by attribute). Lists are changeable, and their items are typically homogenous, thus they may be accessed by iterating over the list.
Note: When unpacking a tuple, the number of variables on the left should be equal to the number of values in the provided tuple a.
# Accessing Tuple
# with Indexing
Tuple1 = tuple("micks")
print("\nFirst element of Tuple: ")
print(Tuple1[0])
# Tuple unpacking
Tuple1 = ("micks", "For", "micks")
# This line unpack
# values of Tuple1
a, b, c = Tuple1
print("\nValues after unpacking: ")
print(a)
print(b)
print(c)
Output:
First element of Tuple:
M
Values after unpacking:
micks
For
micks
Complexities for accessing elements in tuples:
Time complexity: O(1)

Space complexity: O(1)

## CONCATENATION OF TUPLES

The technique of connecting two or more Tuples is known as tuple concatenation. Concatenation is accomplished with the use of the '+' operator. Tuple concatenation is always performed from the end of the original tuple. Tuples do not support any other arithmetic operations.
Only the same datatypes can be concatenated using concatenation; combining a list and a tuple results in an error.

```
# Concatenation of tuples
Tuple1 = (0, 1, 2, 3)
Tuple2 = ('micks', 'For', 'micks')
Tuple3 = Tuple1 + Tuple2
# Printing first Tuple
print("Tuple 1: ")
print(Tuple1)
# Printing Second Tuple
print("\nTuple2: ")
print(Tuple2)
# Printing Final Tuple
print("\nTuples after Concatenation: ")
print(Tuple3)
Output:
Tuple 1:
(0, 1, 2, 3)
Tuple2:
('micks', 'For', 'micks')
Tuples after Concatenation:
(0, 1, 2, 3, 'micks', 'For', 'micks')
Time Complexity: O(1)
Auxiliary Space: O(1)
```

## SLICING OF TUPLE

Tuple slicing is used to retrieve a specified range or slice of sub-elements from a Tuple. Slicing is also possible with lists and arrays. Indexing in a list returns a single element, whereas Slicing returns a collection of items. Negative Increment values can also be used to reverse the Tuple sequence.

| M | I | C | H | E | A | L | M | I | C | K |
|---|---|---|---|---|---|---|---|---|---|---|
| 0 | 1 | 2 | 3 | 4 | 5 | 6 | 7 | 8 | 9 | 10 |
| -11 | -10 | -9 | -8 | -7 | -6 | -5 | -4 | -3 | -2 | -1 |

```
# Slicing of a Tuple
# Slicing of a Tuple
# with Numbers
Tuple1 = tuple('MICHEALMICK')
# Removing the First element
print("Removal of First Element: ")
print(Tuple1[1:])
# Reversing the Tuple
print("\nTuple after sequence of Element is reversed: ")
print(Tuple1[::-1])
# Printing elements of a Range
print("\nPrinting elements between Range 4-9: ")
print(Tuple1[4:9])
```

Output:
Removal of First Element:
('I', 'C', 'H', 'E', 'A', 'L', 'M', 'I', 'C', 'K')
Tuple after sequence of Element is reversed:
('K', 'C', 'I', 'M', 'L', 'A', 'E', 'H', 'C', 'I', 'M')
Printing elements between Range 4-9:
('E', 'A', 'L', 'M', 'I')

## DELETING A TUPLE

Tuples is immutable, therefore deleting a portion of it is not possible. The del() function is used to remove the whole tuple. Note: Printing Tuple after deletion causes an error.

```
# Deleting a Tuple
Tuple1 = (0, 1, 2, 3, 4)
del Tuple1
print(Tuple1)
Traceback (most recent call last):
File "/home/efa50fd0709dec08434191f32275928a.py", line 7, in
print(Tuple1)
NameError: name 'Tuple1' is not defined
```

## BUILT-IN METHODS

| Built-in-Method | Description |
|---|---|
| index( ) | Finds the provided value in the tuple and returns the index where it is found. |
| count( ) | The frequency of occurrence of a specific value is returned. |

## BUILT-IN FUNCTIONS

| Built-in Function | Description |
|---|---|
| all() | Returns true if all elements are true, or true if any element in the tuple is true if the tuple is empty. Return false if the tuple is empty. |
| any() | Returns the length or size of the tuple. |
| len() | Returns an enumerate tuple object. |
| enumerate() | return the most significant member of the provided tuple |
| max() | yield the smallest member of the supplied tuple |
| min() | Sums the integers in the tuple input elements and returns a new sorted list |
| sum() | Convert a list to a tuple. |
| sorted() | Returns true if all elements are true, or true if any element in the tuple is true if the tuple is empty. Return false if the tuple is empty. |
| tuple() | Returns the length or size of the tuple. |

## TUPLES VS LISTS
### SIMILARITIES

Functions that can be used for both lists and tuples:
len(), max(), min(), sum(), any(), all(), sorted()
Methods that can be used for both lists and tuples:
count(), Index()
Tuples can be stored in lists.
Lists can be stored in tuples.
Both 'tuples' and 'lists' can be nested.


# *DIFFERENCES*


Methods that cannot be used for tuples:
append(), insert(), remove(), pop(), clear(), sort(), reverse()
we generally use 'tuples' for heterogeneous (different) data types and 'lists'
for homogeneous (similar) data types.
Iterating through a 'tuple' is faster than in a 'list'.
'Lists' are mutable whereas 'tuples' are immutable.
Tuples that contain immutable elements can be used as a key for a
dictionary.

# CHAPTER SEVEN: UNDERSTANDING PYTHON SETS

A Set in Python is an unordered collection of data types that is iterable, changeable, and does not contain duplicate entries. The order of the items in a set is unknown, yet it may contain several elements. The main advantage of utilizing a set over a list is that it provides a highly efficient way for determining if a certain member is in the set.

## CREATING A SET

Sets may be formed by using the built-in set() method with an iterable object or a sequence enclosed in curly braces separated by a 'comma'. Because a set is changeable, it cannot have mutable items like a list or dictionary.

```
# Python program to demonstrate
# Creation of Set in Python
# Creating a Set
set1 = set()
print("Initial blank Set: ")
print(set1)
# Creating a Set with
# the use of a String
set1 = set("micksformicks")
print("\nSet with the use of String: ")
print(set1)
# Creating a Set with
# the use of Constructor
# (Using object to Store String)
String = 'micksformicks'
set1 = set(String)
print("\nSet with the use of an Object: " )
print(set1)
# Creating a Set with
# the use of a List
set1 = set(["micks", "For", "micks"])
print("\nSet with the use of List: ")
print(set1)
Output
Initial blank Set:
set()
Set with the use of String:
```

{'r', 's', 'o', 'F', 'm', 'k', 'c'}
Set with the use of an Object:
{'r', 's', 'o', 'F', 'm', 'k', 'c'}

Set with the use of List:
{'For', 'mickks'}
O(n) is the time complexity, where n is the length of the input string or list.
O(n), where n is the length of the input string or list, because the size of the set formed is dependent on the size of the input.

A set has only unique components, however numerous duplicate values can be given while creating the set. The order of items in a set is undefined and cannot be changed. A set's elements do not have to be of the same type; other mixed-up data type values can also be provided to the set.

```
# Creating a Set with
# a List of Numbers
# (Having duplicate values)
set1 = set([1, 2, 4, 4, 3, 3, 3, 6, 5])
print("\nSet with the use of Numbers: ")
print(set1)
# Creating a Set with
# a mixed type of values
# (Having numbers and strings)
set1 = set([1, 2, 'micks', 4, 'For', 6, 'mickks'])
print("\nSet with the use of Mixed Values")
print(set1)
```

Output
Set with the use of Numbers:
{1, 2, 3, 4, 5, 6}
Set with the use of Mixed Values
{1, 2, 4, 6, 'micks', 'For'}
Creating a set with another method

```
# Another Method to create sets in Python3
# Set containing numbers
my_set = {1, 2, 3}
print(my_set)
# This code is contributed by micheal
```

Output
{1, 2, 3}

## ADDING ELEMENTS TO A SET

Using add() method
The built-in add() method can be used to add elements to the Set. The add() function can only add one element to the set at a time; loops are used to add numerous pieces at once with the add() method.

Note that lists cannot be added as elements to a set because they are not hashable, however tuples may be added because they are immutable and hence hashable.

```
# Python program to demonstrate
# Addition of elements in a Set
# Creating a Set
set1 = set()
print("Initial blank Set: ")
print(set1)
# Adding element and tuple to the Set
set1.add(8)
set1.add(9)
set1.add((6, 7))
print("\nSet after Addition of Three elements: ")
print(set1)
# Adding elements to the Set
# using Iterator
for i in range(1, 6):
 set1.add(i)
print("\nSet after Addition of elements from 1-5: ")
print(set1)
```

Output
Initial blank Set:
set()
Set after Addition of Three elements:
{8, 9, (6, 7)}
Set after Addition of elements from 1-5:
{1, 2, 3, (6, 7), 4, 5, 8, 9}

Using update() method
The Update() function is used to add two or more components. The update() function accepts as inputs lists, strings, tuples, and other collections. Duplicate items are avoided in all of these scenarios.

```
# Python program to demonstrate
# Addition of elements in a Set
```

```
# Addition of elements to the Set
# using Update function
set1 = set([4, 5, (6, 7)])
set1.update([10, 11])
print("\nSet after Addition of elements using Update: ")
print(set1)
Output
Set after Addition of elements using Update:
{4, 5, (6, 7), 10, 11}
```

## ACCESSING A SET

Set items cannot be retrieved using an index because sets are unordered and the elements have no index. However, you may use a for loop to cycle over the set elements, or the in keyword to query if a specific value is contained in a set.

```
# Python program to demonstrate
# Accessing of elements in a set
# Creating a set
set1 = set(["micks", "For", "micks"])
print("\nInitial set")
print(set1)
# Accessing element using
# for loop
print("\nElements of set: ")
for i in set1:
 print(i, end=" ")
# Checking the element
# using in keyword
print("micks" in set1)
Output
Initial set
{'micks', 'For'}
Elements of set:
Micks For True
```

## REMOVING ELEMENTS FROM THE SET

Using remove() method or discard() method:
Elements can be deleted from the Set using the built-in remove() method, however if the element does not exist in the set, a KeyError is thrown. Use

132

discard() to delete entries from a set without raising a KeyError; if the element does not exist in the set, it remains unaffected.

```python
# Python program to demonstrate
# Deletion of elements in a Set
# Creating a Set
set1 = set([1, 2, 3, 4, 5, 6,
   7, 8, 9, 10, 11, 12])
print("Initial Set: ")
print(set1)
# Removing elements from Set
# using Remove() method
set1.remove(5)
set1.remove(6)
print("\nSet after Removal of two elements: ")
print(set1)
# Removing elements from Set
# using Discard() method
set1.discard(8)
set1.discard(9)
print("\nSet after Discarding two elements: ")
print(set1)
# Removing elements from Set
# using iterator method
for i in range(1, 5):
 set1.remove(i)
print("\nSet after Removing a range of elements: ")
print(set1)
```

Output

Initial Set:

{1, 2, 3, 4, 5, 6, 7, 8, 9, 10, 11, 12}

Set after Removal of two elements:

{1, 2, 3, 4, 7, 8, 9, 10, 11, 12}

Set after Discarding two elements:

{1, 2, 3, 4, 7, 10, 11, 12}

Set after Removing a range of elements:

{7, 10, 11, 12}

Using pop() method:

The Pop() method may also be used to remove and return one element from a set, however it only removes the set's final element.

There is no way to know which element gets popped by using the pop() method if the set is unordered.

```
# Python program to demonstrate
# Deletion of elements in a Set
# Creating a Set
set1 = set([1, 2, 3, 4, 5, 6,
    7, 8, 9, 10, 11, 12])
print("Initial Set: ")
print(set1)
# Removing element from the
# Set using the pop() method
set1.pop()
print("\nSet after popping an element: ")
print(set1)
Output
Initial Set:
{1, 2, 3, 4, 5, 6, 7, 8, 9, 10, 11, 12}
Set after popping an element:
{2, 3, 4, 5, 6, 7, 8, 9, 10, 11, 12}
```

Using clear() method:

To remove all the elements from the set, clear() function is used.

```
#Creating a set
set1 = set([1,2,3,4,5])
print("\n Initial set: ")
print(set1)
# Removing all the elements from
# Set using clear() method
set1.clear()
print("\nSet after clearing all the elements: ")
print(set1)
Output
 Initial set:
{1, 2, 3, 4, 5}
Set after clearing all the elements:
set()
```

In Python, frozen sets are immutable objects that only support methods and operators that yield a result without changing the frozen set or sets to which they are applied. While parts of a set can be changed at any moment, elements of a frozen set do not change after they are created. It returns an empty frozenset if no arguments are supplied.

```
# Python program to demonstrate
# working of a FrozenSet
# Creating a Set
```

```python
String = ('m', 'i', 'c', 'k', 's', 'F', 'o', 'r')
Fset1 = frozenset(String)
print("The FrozenSet is: ")
print(Fset1)
# To print Empty Frozen Set
# No parameter is passed
print("\nEmpty FrozenSet: ")
print(frozenset())
```
Output
The FrozenSet is:
frozenset({'F', 's', 'o', 'm', 'r', 'i', 'k'})
Empty FrozenSet:
frozenset()
Typecasting Objects into sets

- # Typecasting Objects in Python3 into sets

# Typecasting list into set

- my_list = [1, 2, 3, 3, 4, 5, 5, 6, 2]
- my_set = set(my_list)
- print("my_list as a set: ", my_set)

# Typecasting string into set

- my_str = "micksformicks"
- my_set1 = set(my_str)
- print("my_str as a set: ", my_set1)

# Typecasting dictionary into set

- my_dict = {1: "One", 2: "Two", 3: "Three"}
- my_set2 = set(my_dict)
- print("my_dict as a set: ", my_set2)
- # This code is contributed by micheal

Output
my_list as a set: {1, 2, 3, 4, 5, 6}
my_str as a set: {'G', 'f', 'r', 'e', 'k', 'o', 's'}
my_dict as a set: {1, 2, 3}
Example: Implementing all functions:
```python
def create_set():
  my_set = {1, 2, 3, 4, 5}
  print(my_set)
```

```python
def add_element():
    my_set = {1, 2, 3, 4, 5}
    my_set.add(6)
    print(my_set)
def remove_element():
    my_set = {1, 2, 3, 4, 5}
    my_set.remove(3)
    print(my_set)
def clear_set():
    my_set = {1, 2, 3, 4, 5}
    my_set.clear()
    print(my_set)
def set_union():
    set1 = {1, 2, 3}
    set2 = {4, 5, 6}
    my_set = set1.union(set2)
    print(my_set)
def set_intersection():
    set1 = {1, 2, 3, 4, 5}
    set2 = {4, 5, 6, 7, 8}
    my_set = set1.intersection(set2)
    print(my_set)
def set_difference():
    set1 = {1, 2, 3, 4, 5}
    set2 = {4, 5, 6, 7, 8}
    my_set = set1.difference(set2)
    print(my_set)
def set_symmetric_difference():
    set1 = {1, 2, 3, 4, 5}
    set2 = {4, 5, 6, 7, 8}
    my_set = set1.symmetric_difference(set2)
    print(my_set)
def set_subset():
    set1 = {1, 2, 3, 4, 5}
    set2 = {2, 3, 4}
    subset = set2.issubset(set1)
    print(subset)
def set_superset():
    set1 = {1, 2, 3, 4, 5}
    set2 = {2, 3, 4}
    superset = set1.issuperset(set2)
```

```
  print(superset)
if __name__ == '__main__':
  create_set()
  add_element()
  remove_element()
  clear_set()
  set_union()
  set_intersection()
  set_difference()
  set_symmetric_difference()
  set_subset()
  set_superset()
```
Output
{1, 2, 3, 4, 5}
{1, 2, 3, 4, 5, 6}
{1, 2, 4, 5}
set()
{1, 2, 3, 4, 5, 6}
{4, 5}
{1, 2, 3}
{1, 2, 3, 6, 7, 8}
True
True

## PROS

Sets may only includes unique components, hence they might be useful for eliminating duplicates from a data collection.

Sets are optimized for rapid membership checking, therefore they can be handy for detecting whether or not a value is in a collection.

Sets allow mathematical set operations such as union, intersection, and difference, which can be beneficial when working with data sets.

Sets are changeable, which means you may add or delete components from them after they've been constructed.

## CONS

Sets in Python are unordered, meaning that the order of data in a set cannot be relied on upon. This lack of order can pose challenges when it comes to accessing or processing the data in a specific sequence, adding an element of complexity to working with sets.

When compared to lists, sets exhibit limited functionality. Unlike lists, sets do not support methods such as append() or pop(), which are commonly used for modifying or manipulating data. Consequently, altering or managing data stored in a set can become more cumbersome.

Memory usage is another aspect to consider when working with sets. Sets tend to consume more memory than lists, particularly for small datasets. This is because each element within a set necessitates additional memory to store a hash value. Therefore, the memory footprint of sets can be relatively larger.

It's worth noting that sets are less frequently utilized in Python compared to lists and dictionaries. As a result, there might be fewer resources or libraries available for working specifically with sets. This scarcity of dedicated support can make it more challenging to find solutions or seek assistance with debugging when working with sets.

Sets can serve as a valuable data structure in Python, particularly for tasks such as eliminating duplicates or swiftly checking membership. However, their unordered nature and limited functionality make them less versatile than lists or dictionaries. Therefore, it is crucial to carefully weigh the advantages and disadvantages of using sets when determining the appropriate data structure for your Python program.

## SET METHODS

| Function | Description |
| --- | --- |
| add() | Adds an element to a set |
| remove() | Removes an element from a set. If the element is not present in the set, raise a KeyError |
| clear() | Removes all elements form a set |
| copy() | Returns a shallow copy of a set |
| pop() | Removes and returns an arbitrary set element. Raise KeyError if the set is empty |
| update() | Updates a set with the |

| | union of itself and others |
|---|---|
| union() | Returns the union of sets in a new set |
| difference() | Returns the difference of two or more sets as a new set |
| difference_update() | Removes all elements of another set from this set |
| discard() | Removes an element from set if it is a member. (Do nothing if the element is not in set) |
| intersection() | Returns the intersection of two sets as a new set |
| intersection_update() | Updates the set with the intersection of itself and another |
| isdisjoint() | Returns True if two sets have a null intersection |
| issubset() | Returns True if another set contains this set |
| issuperset() | Returns True if this set contains another set |
| symmetric_difference() | Returns the symmetric difference of two sets as a new set |
| symmetric_difference_update() | Updates a set with the symmetric difference of itself and another |

# CHAPTER EIGHT: UNDERSTANDING PYTHON DICTIONARY

In Python, a dictionary is a collection of keys and values that is used to store data values like a map, as opposed to other data types that only carry a single value as an element.

## EXAMPLE OF DICTIONARY IN PYTHON

A dictionary has a key:value pair. To make the dictionary more optimized, Key-Value is supplied.
Dict = {1: 'micks', 2: 'For', 3: 'micks'}
print(Dict)
Output:
{1: 'micks', 2: 'For', 3: 'micks'}

## CREATING A DICTIONARY

A dictionary may be built in Python by putting a sequence of entries between curly braces and separated by a 'comma'. Dictionary stores pairs of values, one of which is the Key and the other being the Key:value pair element. A dictionary's values can be of any data type and can be replicated, however keys cannot be copied and must be immutable.
Dictionary keys are case sensitive; the same name but various Key cases will be treated differently.
# Creating a Dictionary
# with Integer Keys
Dict = {1: 'micks', 2: 'For', 3: 'micks'}
print("\nDictionary with the use of Integer Keys: ")
print(Dict)
# Creating a Dictionary
# with Mixed keys
Dict = {'Name': 'micks', 1: [1, 2, 3, 4]}
print("\nDictionary with the use of Mixed Keys: ")
print(Dict)
Output:
Dictionary with the use of Integer Keys:
{1: 'micks', 2: 'For', 3: 'micks'}
Dictionary with the use of Mixed Keys:
{'Name': 'micks', 1: [1, 2, 3, 4]}
Dictionary can also be created by the built-in function dict(). An empty dictionary can be created by just placing to curly braces{}.

```
# Creating an empty Dictionary
Dict = {}
print("Empty Dictionary: ")
print(Dict)
# Creating a Dictionary
# with dict() method
Dict = dict({1: 'micks', 2: 'For', 3: 'micks'})
print("\nDictionary with the use of dict(): ")
print(Dict)
# Creating a Dictionary
# with each item as a Pair
Dict = dict([(1, 'micks'), (2, 'For')])
print("\nDictionary with each item as a pair: ")
print(Dict)
```
Output:
Empty Dictionary:
{}
Dictionary with the use of dict():
{1: 'micks', 2: 'For', 3: 'micks'}
Dictionary with each item as a pair:
{1: 'micks', 2: 'For'}
Complexities for Creating a Dictionary:
Time complexity: O(len(dict))
Space complexity: O(n)

## NESTED DICTIONARY

```
# Creating a Nested Dictionary
# as shown in the below image
Dict = {1: 'micks', 2: 'For',
    3: {'A': 'Welcome', 'B': 'To', 'C': 'micks'}}
print(Dict)
```
Output:
{1: 'micks', 2: 'For', 3: {'A': 'Welcome', 'B': 'To', 'C': 'micks'}}

## ADDING ELEMENTS TO A DICTIONARY

Elements can be added in a variety of ways. By declaring value together with the key, for example, Dict[Key] = 'Value', one value at a time may be added to a Dictionary. The built-in update() function may be used to update an existing value in a Dictionary. An existing Dictionary can also have nested key values added to it.

Note: If the key-value pair already exists, the value is changed; otherwise, a new Key with the value is added to the Dictionary.

```
# Creating an empty Dictionary
Dict = {}
print("Empty Dictionary: ")
print(Dict)
# Adding elements one at a time
Dict[0] = 'micks'
Dict[2] = 'For'
Dict[3] = 1
print("\nDictionary after adding 3 elements: ")
print(Dict)
# Adding set of values
# to a single Key
Dict['Value_set'] = 2, 3, 4
print("\nDictionary after adding 3 elements: ")
print(Dict)
# Updating existing Key's Value
Dict[2] = 'Welcome'
print("\nUpdated key value: ")
print(Dict)
# Adding Nested Key value to Dictionary
Dict[5] = {'Nested': {'1': 'Life', '2': 'micks'}}
print("\nAdding a Nested Key: ")
print(Dict)
```

Output:
Empty Dictionary:
{}
Dictionary after adding 3 elements:
{0: 'micks', 2: 'For', 3: 1}
Dictionary after adding 3 elements:
{0: 'micks', 2: 'For', 3: 1, 'Value_set': (2, 3, 4)}
Updated key value:
{0: 'micks', 2: 'Welcome', 3: 1, 'Value_set': (2, 3, 4)}
Adding a Nested Key:
{0: 'micks', 2: 'Welcome', 3: 1, 'Value_set': (2, 3, 4), 5:
{'Nested': {'1': 'Life', '2': 'micks'}}}
Complexities for Adding elements in a Dictionary:
Time complexity: O(1)/O(n)
Space complexity: O(1)

## ACCESSING ELEMENTS OF A DICTIONARY

Refer to a dictionary's key name to access its elements. Key can be used inside square brackets.

```
# Python program to demonstrate
# accessing a element from a Dictionary
# Creating a Dictionary
Dict = {1: 'micks', 'name': 'For', 3: 'micks'}
# accessing a element using key
print("Accessing a element using key:")
print(Dict['name'])

# accessing a element using key
print("Accessing a element using key:")
print(Dict[1])
```

Output:

Accessing a element using key:

For

Accessing a element using key:

micks

There is also a function named get() that may be used to obtain an element from a dictionary.This method takes a key as an input and returns a value.

Complexities for Accessing elements in a Dictionary:

Time complexity: $O(1)$

Space complexity: $O(1)$

```
# Creating a Dictionary
Dict = {1: 'micks', 'name': 'For', 3: 'micks'}
# accessing a element using get()
# method
print("Accessing an element using get:")
print(Dict.get(3))
```

Output:

Accessing an element using get:

Micks

## ACCESSING AN ELEMENT OF A NESTED DICTIONARY

Use indexing [] syntax to get the value of any key in the nested dictionary.
# Creating a Dictionary
Dict = {'Dict1': {1: 'micks'},
  'Dict2': {'Name': 'For'}}
# Accessing element using key
print(Dict['Dict1'])
print(Dict['Dict1'][1])
print(Dict['Dict2']['Name'])
Output:
{1: 'micks'}
micks
For

## DELETING ELEMENTS USING DEL KEYWORD

The dictionary items can be erased with the del keyword, as seen below.

```
# Python program to demonstrate
# Deleting Elements using del Keyword
# Creating a Dictionary
Dict = {1: 'micks', 'name': 'For', 3: 'micks'}
print("Dictionary =")
print(Dict)
#Deleting some of the Dictionar data
del(Dict[1])
print("Data after deletion Dictionary=")
print(Dict)
Output
Dictionary ={1: 'micks', 'name': 'For', 3: 'micks'}
Data after deletion Dictionary={'name': 'For', 3: 'micks'}
```

## DICTIONARY METHODS

| Method | Description |
|---|---|
| dic.clear() | Remove all the elements from the dictionary |
| dict.copy() | Returns a copy of the dictionary |
| dict.get(key, default = "None") | Returns the value of specified key |
| dict.items() | Returns a list containing a tuple for each key value pair |
| dict.keys() | Returns a list containing dictionary's keys |
| dict.update(dict2) | Updates dictionary with specified key-value pairs |
| dict.values() | Returns a list of all the values of dictionary |
| pop() | Remove the element with specified key |
| popItem() | Removes the last inserted key-value pair |
| dict.setdefault(key,default= "None") | set the key to the default value if the key is not |

146

| | specified in the dictionary |
|---|---|
| dict.has_key(key) | returns true if the dictionary contains the specified key. |
| dict.get(key, default = "None") | used to get the value specified for the passed key. |

```
# demo for all dictionary methods
dict1 = {1: "Python", 2: "Java", 3: "Ruby", 4: "Scala"}
# copy() method
dict2 = dict1.copy()
print(dict2)
# clear() method
dict1.clear()
print(dict1)
# get() method
print(dict2.get(1))
# items() method
print(dict2.items())
# keys() method
print(dict2.keys())
# pop() method
dict2.pop(4)
print(dict2)
# popitem() method
dict2.popitem()
print(dict2)
# update() method
dict2.update({3: "Scala"})
print(dict2)
# values() method
print(dict2.values())
Output:
{1: 'Python', 2: 'Java', 3: 'Ruby', 4: 'Scala'}
{}
Python
dict_items([(1, 'Python'), (2, 'Java'), (3, 'Ruby'), (4, 'Scala')])
dict_keys([1, 2, 3, 4])
{1: 'Python', 2: 'Java', 3: 'Ruby'}
```

```
{1: 'Python', 2: 'Java'}
{1: 'Python', 2: 'Java', 3: 'Scala'}
dict_values(['Python', 'Java', 'Scala'])
```

# CHAPTER NINE: PYTHON ARRAYS

An array is a fascinating data structure that holds a collection of items, neatly arranged in consecutive memory slots. The brilliance lies in organizing multiple elements of identical nature in a cohesive manner, simplifying the process of determining the exact position of each element. Achieving this feat is as effortless as adding a calculated offset to a base value, which happens to be the memory address of the array's inaugural element, often represented by the array's name.

Let's take a moment to visualize an array as a vibrant staircase, teeming with vitality. Picture each step accommodating a unique value, perhaps symbolizing one of your cherished friends. Now, isn't it remarkable that by merely knowing the step count, you can effortlessly pinpoint the whereabouts of any of your dear companions? Such is the power of arrays.

In the realm of Python, arrays gracefully reveal themselves through a module aptly named "array." This handy tool serves as a conduit for managing arrays and unlocks their potential. Notably, arrays shine brightest when we need to handle data of a specific type exclusively. Interestingly, users can treat lists as arrays, but alas, they lack the ability to enforce strict element type constraints. However, fear not, for the array module presents itself as a panacea. With this magical module, all the elements within an array must conform harmoniously to the same data type, promoting order and harmony.

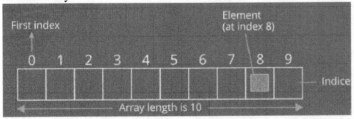

## CREATING AN ARRAY

Importing the array module in Python allows you to build an array. array(data_type, value_list) constructs an array using the data type and value list parameters.

```
# Python program to demonstrate
# Creation of Array
# importing "array" for array creations
import array as arr
# creating an array with integer type
a = arr.array('i', [1, 2, 3])
```

```
# printing original array
print("The new created array is : ", end=" ")
for i in range(0, 3):
 print(a[i], end=" ")
print()

# creating an array with double type
b = arr.array('d', [2.5, 3.2, 3.3])
# printing original array
print("\nThe new created array is : ", end=" ")
for i in range(0, 3):
 print(b[i], end=" ")
```

Output :

The new created array is :  1 2 3

The new created array is :  2.5 3.2 3.3

Complexities for Creation of Arrays:

Time Complexity: O(1)

Auxiliary Space: O(n)

Some of the data types that will be useful in generating an array of diverse data kinds are listed below.

| Type Code | C Type | Python Type | Maximum Size in Bytes |
|---|---|---|---|
| 'b' | signed char | int | 1 |
| 'B' | unsigned char | int | 1 |
| 'u' | Py_UNICODE | unicode character | 2 |
| 'h' | signed short | int | 2 |
| 'H' | unsigned short | int | 2 |
| 'i' | signed int | int | 2 |
| 'I' | unsigned int | int | 2 |
| 'l' | signed long | int | 4 |
| 'L' | unsigned long | int | 4 |
| 'q' | signed long long | int | 8 |
| 'Q' | unsigned long long | int | 8 |
| 'f' | float | float | 4 |
| 'd' | double | float | 8 |

## ADDING ELEMENTS TO AN ARRAY

The built-in insert() method may be used to add elements to the Array. Insert is a function that is used to insert one or more data elements into an array. A new element can be inserted at the beginning, end, or any provided index of the array depending on the necessity. append() may also be used to append the value specified in its arguments to the end of an array.

```
# Python program to demonstrate
# Adding Elements to an Array
# importing "array" for array creations
import array as arr
# array with int type
a = arr.array('i', [1, 2, 3])
print("Array before insertion : ", end=" ")
for i in range(0, 3):
    print(a[i], end=" ")
print()
# inserting array using
# insert() function
a.insert(1, 4)
print("Array after insertion : ", end=" ")
for i in (a):
    print(i, end=" ")
print()
# array with float type
b = arr.array('d', [2.5, 3.2, 3.3])
print("Array before insertion : ", end=" ")
for i in range(0, 3):
    print(b[i], end=" ")
print()
# adding an element using append()
b.append(4.4)
print("Array after insertion : ", end=" ")
for i in (b):
    print(i, end=" ")
print()
```
Output
Array before insertion :  1 2 3
Array after insertion :  1 4 2 3
Array before insertion :  2.5 3.2 3.3
Array after insertion :  2.5 3.2 3.3 4.4

Complexities for Adding elements to the Arrays:
Time Complexity: O(1)/O(n) ( O(1) – for inserting elements at the end of the array, O(n) – for inserting elements at the beginning of the array and to the full array
Auxiliary Space: O(1)

## ACCESSING ELEMENTS FROM THE ARRAY

Refer to the index number to access the array entries. To retrieve an item in an array, use the index operator []. The index must be a positive integer.

```
# Python program to demonstrate
# accessing of element from list
# importing array module
import array as arr
# array with int type
a = arr.array('i', [1, 2, 3, 4, 5, 6])
# accessing element of array
print("Access element is: ", a[0])
# accessing element of array
print("Access element is: ", a[3])
# array with float type
b = arr.array('d', [2.5, 3.2, 3.3])
# accessing element of array
print("Access element is: ", b[1])
# accessing element of array
print("Access element is: ", b[2])
Output
Access element is:  1
Access element is:  4
Access element is:  3.2
Access element is:  3.3
```

Complexities for accessing elements in the Arrays:
Time Complexity: O(1)
Auxiliary Space: O(1)

## REMOVING ELEMENTS FROM THE ARRAY

Elements in the array can be deleted using the built-in remove() method, however an error occurs if the element does not exist in the set. The Remove() function only removes one element at a time; an iterator is needed to remove a range of elements.

152

The pop() function may also be used to remove and return an element from an array, but by default it only removes the final element of the array; to remove an element from a specified place in the array, supply the index of the element as an argument to the pop() method.

Please keep in mind that the delete function in List will only delete the first occurrence of the searched element.

```python
# Python program to demonstrate
# Removal of elements in an Array
# importing "array" for array operations
import array
# initializing array with array values
# initializes array with signed integers
arr = array.array('i', [1, 2, 3, 1, 5])
# printing original array
print("The new created array is : ", end="")
for i in range(0, 5):
 print(arr[i], end=" ")
print("\r")
# using pop() to remove element at 2nd position
print("The popped element is : ", end="")
print(arr.pop(2))
# printing array after popping
print("The array after popping is : ", end="")
for i in range(0, 4):
 print(arr[i], end=" ")

print("\r")
# using remove() to remove 1st occurrence of 1
arr.remove(1)
# printing array after removing
print("The array after removing is : ", end="")
for i in range(0, 3):
 print(arr[i], end=" ")
```

Output:
The new created array is : 1 2 3 1 5
The popped element is : 3
The array after popping is : 1 2 1 5
The array after removing is : 2 1 5
Complexities for Removing elements in the Arrays:

Time Complexity: O(1)/O(n) ( O(1) – for removing elements at the end of the array, O(n) – for removing elements at the beginning of the array and to the full array
Auxiliary Space: O(1)

## SLICING OF AN ARRAY

There are other ways to print the entire array with all of its elements in Python, but we utilize the Slice operation to display a selected range of elements from the array. The slice operation is done on the array using the colon(:). To print items from the beginning to the end of a range, use [:Index], to print elements from the beginning to the end of a range, use [:-Index], to print elements from a specific Index to the end, use [Index:], to print elements inside a range, use [Start Index:End Index], and to print the whole List using the slicing operation, use [:]. Use [::-1] to print the entire array in reverse order.

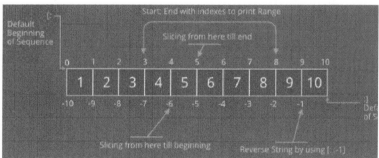

```
# Python program to demonstrate
# slicing of elements in an Array
# importing array module
import array as arr
# creating a list
l = [1, 2, 3, 4, 5, 6, 7, 8, 9, 10]
a = arr.array('i', l)
print("Initial Array: ")
for i in (a):
 print(i, end=" ")
# Print elements of a range
# using Slice operation
Sliced_array = a[3:8]
print("\nSlicing elements in a range 3-8: ")
print(Sliced_array)
```

154

```python
# Print elements from a
# pre-defined point to end
Sliced_array = a[5:]
print("\nElements sliced from 5th "
 "element till the end: ")
print(Sliced_array)
# Printing elements from
# beginning till end
Sliced_array = a[:]
print("\nPrinting all elements using slice operation: ")
print(Sliced_array)
```
Output
Initial Array:
1 2 3 4 5 6 7 8 9 10
Slicing elements in a range 3-8:
array('i', [4, 5, 6, 7, 8])
Elements sliced from 5th element till the end:
array('i', [6, 7, 8, 9, 10])

Printing all elements using slice operation:
array('i', [1, 2, 3, 4, 5, 6, 7, 8, 9, 10])

## SEARCHING AN ELEMENT IN AN ARRAY

To find an entry in an array, we utilize the index() function included into Python. This function returns the index of the first instance of the value specified in the parameters.

```python
# Python code to demonstrate
# searching an element in array
# importing array module
import array
# initializing array with array values
# initializes array with signed integers
arr = array.array('i', [1, 2, 3, 1, 2, 5])
# printing original array
print("The new created array is : ", end="")
for i in range(0, 6):
 print(arr[i], end=" ")
print("\r")
# using index() to print index of 1st occurrence of 2
print("The index of 1st occurrence of 2 is : ", end="")
```

```
print(arr.index(2))

# using index() to print index of 1st occurrence of 1
print("The index of 1st occurrence of 1 is : ", end="")
print(arr.index(1))
Output
The new created array is : 1 2 3 1 2 5
The index of 1st occurrence of 2 is : 1
The index of 1st occurrence of 1 is : 0
Complexities for searching elements in the Arrays:
Time Complexity: O(n)
Auxiliary Space: O(1)
```

## UPDATING ELEMENTS IN AN ARRAY

To update an array element, just assign a new value to the index that needs to be updated.

```
# Python code to demonstrate
# how to update an element in array
# importing array module
import array
# initializing array with array values
# initializes array with signed integers
arr = array.array('i', [1, 2, 3, 1, 2, 5])
# printing original array
print("Array before updation : ", end="")
for i in range(0, 6):
 print(arr[i], end=" ")
print("\r")
# updating an element inana array
arr[2] = 6
print("Array after updation : ", end="")
for i in range(0, 6):
 print(arr[i], end=" ")
print()
# updating an element inana array
arr[4] = 8
print("Array after updation : ", end="")
for i in range(0, 6):
 print(arr[i], end=" ")
Output
```

Array before updation : 1 2 3 1 2 5
Array after updation : 1 2 6 1 2 5
Array after updation : 1 2 6 1 8 5
Complexities for updating elements in the Arrays:
Time Complexity: O(n)
Auxiliary Space: O(1)

## COUNTING ELEMENTS IN AN ARRAY

To count the items in an array, we must use the count method.

```
import array
# Create an array of integers
my_array = array.array('i', [1, 2, 3, 4, 2, 5, 2])
# Count the number of occurrences of the element 2 in the array
count = my_array.count(2)
# Print the result
print("Number of occurrences of 2:", count)
```

Output

Number of occurrences of 2: 3

Complexities for counting elements in the Arrays:
Time Complexity: O(n)
Auxiliary Space: O(1)

## REVERSING ELEMENTS IN AN ARRAY

To reverse the items in an array, we simply use the reverse method.

```
import array
# Create an array of integers
my_array = array.array('i', [1, 2, 3, 4, 5])
# Print the original array
print("Original array:", *my_array)

# Reverse the array in place
my_array.reverse()
# Print the reversed array
print("Reversed array:", *my_array)
```

Output

Original array: 1 2 3 4 5

Reversed array: 5 4 3 2 1

Complexities for reversing elements in the Arrays:
Time Complexity: O(n)
Space: O(1)

157

## EXTEND ELEMENT FROM ARRAY

We will look at the Python list extend() function and try to comprehend it.

### WHAT IS AN EXTENDED ELEMENT FROM AN ARRAY?

Python employs arrays as a means to retain numerous values or elements sharing the same datatype within a solitary variable. The extend() function, in essence, serves to append an item from an iterable to the array's tail end. Put plainly, this method enables the addition of an array brimming with values to an established or preexisting array, thereby augmenting its magnitude.

Syntax of list extend()
The syntax of the extend() method:
list.extend(iterable)
Here,all the element of iterable are added to the end of list1
Example 1:

```
#Python program to demonstrate
# Adding Elements to an Array
# importing "array" for array creations
import array as arr
# array with int type
a = arr.array('i', [1, 2, 3,4,5])
#printing original array
print("The before array extend : ", end =" ")
for i in range (0, 5):
 print (a[i], end =" ")
print()
#creating an array with using extend method
a.extend([6,7,8,9,10])
#printing original array
print("\nThe array after extend :",end=" ")
for i in range(0,10):

 print(a[i],end=" ")
print()
```

Output
The before array extend  :  1 2 3 4 5
The array after extend : 1 2 3 4 5 6 7 8 9 10
Example 2:

```python
#Python program to demonstrate
# Creation of Array
# importing "array" for array creations
import array as arr
#creating an array with integer type
a=arr.array('i',[1,2,3,4,5,6])
# printing original array
print("The Before extend array is :",end=" ")
for i in range(0,6):
 print(a[i],end=" ")
print()
# creating an array with using extend method
a.extend([7,8,9,10,11,12])
# printing original array
print("\nThe After extend array is :",end=" ")

for i in range(0,12):
 print(a[i],end=" ")
print()
#array with float type
b = arr.array('d', [2.1,2.2,2.3,2.4,2.5,2.6])
print("\nThe before extend array is :",end=" ")
for i in range(0,6):
print(b[i],end=" ")
print()
#extend function using pass the elements
b.extend([2.6,2.7,2.8,2.9])
print("\nThe after extend array is :",end=" ")
for i in range(0,9+1):
print(b[i],end=" ")
print()
```
Output
The Before extend array is : 1 2 3 4 5 6
The After extend array is : 1 2 3 4 5 6 7 8 9 10 11 12
The before extend array is : 2.1 2.2 2.3 2.4 2.5 2.6
The after extend array is : 2.1 2.2 2.3 2.4 2.5 2.6 2.6 2.7 2.8 2.9

# CHAPTER TEN: CLASSES AND OBJECTS

Python is a computer language that is object-oriented. In Python, almost everything is an object with attributes and functions. A Class functions similarly to an object constructor or a "blueprint" for constructing things.

## CREATE A CLASS

To create a class, use the keyword class:
Example
Create a class named MyClass, with a property named x:
class MyClass:
  x = 5

## CREATE OBJECT

Now we can use the class named MyClass to create objects:
Example
Create an object named p1, and print the value of x:
p1 = MyClass()
print(p1.x)

## THE __INIT__() FUNCTION

The examples above are classes and objects in their most basic form, and thus are not particularly helpful in real-world applications. To comprehend the concept of classes, we must first comprehend the built-in __init__() method. Every class has a procedure called __init__() that is always invoked when the class is launched. Use the __init__() method to assign values to object attributes or to do other activities required when the object is created:
Example
Make a Person class and use the __init__() method to assign values for name and age:
class Person:
  def __init__(self, name, age):
    self.name = name
    self.age = age
p1 = Person("John", 36)
print(p1.name)
print(p1.age)

## THE __STR__() FUNCTION

When a class object is represented as a string, the __str__() method determines what should be returned. If the __str__() function is not set, the object's string representation is returned:

Example

The string representation of an object WITHOUT the __str__() function:

```
class Person:
  def __init__(self, name, age):
    self.name = name
    self.age = age
p1 = Person("John", 36)
print(p1)
```

Example

The string representation of an object WITH the __str__() function:

```
class Person:
  def __init__(self, name, age):
    self.name = name
    self.age = age
  def __str__(self):
    return f"{self.name}({self.age})"
p1 = Person("John", 36)
print(p1)
```

## OBJECT METHODS

Methods can also be found in objects. Object methods are functions that belong to the object. Let's add a function to the Person class:

Example

Insert and run the following function on the p1 object to print a greeting:

```
class Person:
  def __init__(self, name, age):
    self.name = name
    self.age = age
  def myfunc(self):
    print("Hello my name is " + self.name)
p1 = Person("John", 36)
p1.myfunc()
```

Note: The self argument is a reference to the current instance of the class and is used to access class variables.

## The self Parameter

The self argument is a reference to the current instance of the class and is used to access class variables. It does not have to be called self; it may be anything you like, but it must be the first argument of any method in the class:

Example

Instead of self, use the terms mysillyobject and abc:

```
class Person:
  def __init__(mysillyobject, name, age):
    mysillyobject.name = name
    mysillyobject.age = age
  def myfunc(abc):
    print("Hello my name is " + abc.name)
p1 = Person("John", 36)
p1.myfunc()
```

## Modify Object Properties

You may change the following attributes of objects:

Example

Set the age of p1 to 40:

```
p1.age = 40
```

## Delete Object Properties

Using the del keyword, you may erase properties on objects:

Example

Remove the p1 object's age property:

```
del p1.age
```

## Delete Objects

Using the del keyword, you may remove objects:

Example

Delete the p1 object:

```
del p1
```

## THE PASS STATEMENT

Class definitions cannot be empty, however if you have a class definition with no content for any reason, use the pass statement to prevent an error.
Example
class Person:
  pass

## EXERCISE

Make a class called MyClass:
MyClass:
  x = 5

# Chapter Eleven: UNDERSTAND THE OPERATORS IN PYTHON

## Logical Operators

In Python, logical operators are used to execute logical operations on variable values. This value can only be true or false. The truth values' results allow us to deduce the criteria. In Python, there are three types of logical operators: logical AND, logical OR, and logical NOT. Keywords or special characters are used to represent operators.

## Arithmetic Operators

Arithmetic Operators execute a variety of arithmetic operations such as addition, subtraction, multiplication, division, %modulus, exponent, and so on. In Python, you may do arithmetic calculations using the eval function, specify variables and compute them, or use functions.

As an example, for arithmetic operators, we will use the two-digit addition formula 4+5=9.

```
x= 4
y= 5
print(x + y)
```

Output:
9

You may also use additional mathematical operators such as multiplication (*), division (/), subtraction (-), and so on.

## Comparison Operators

Operators of Comparison Python compares the values on both sides of the operand and find their relationship. It is also known as relational operators. Python's comparison operators include (==,!=, >, >,=, and so on).

Example: We will compare the value of x to the value of y and report the result as true or false for comparison operators. In this case, our value of x = 4 is less than y = 5, thus when we display the result as x>y, it really compares the value of x to y and returns false since it is incorrect.

```
x = 4
y = 5
print(('x > y  is',x>y))
```

Output:

('x > y is', False)

Likewise, you can try other comparison operators (x < y, x==y, x!=y, etc.)

## PYTHON ASSIGNMENT OPERATORS

In Python, assignment operators are used to assign the value of the right operand to the left operand. Python's assignment operators include (+=, - =, *=, /=, and so on).

Example: The purpose of Python assignment operators is to simply assign a value, for example.

```
num1 = 4
num2 = 5
print(("Line 1 - Value of num1 : ", num1))
print(("Line 2 - Value of num2 : ", num2))
```

Output :

('Line 1 - Value of num1 : ', 4)

('Line 2 - Value of num2 : ', 5)

Example of compound assignment operator

In the realm of programming, a handy tool at our disposal is the compound assignment operator. This nifty operator grants us the ability to perform arithmetic operations, such as addition, subtraction, or multiplication, on the right operand and subsequently assign the result to the left operand. Essentially, it enables us to combine both the calculation and assignment steps into a single succinct expression, streamlining our code and enhancing efficiency.

Step 1: Assign value to num1 and num2

Step 2: Add value of num1 and num2 (4+5=9)

Step 3: To this result add num1 to the output of Step 2 ( 9+4)

Step 4: It will print the final result as 13

```
num1 = 4
num2 = 5
res = num1 + num2
res += num1
print(("Line 1 - Result of + is ", res))
```

Output :

('Line 1 - Result of + is ', 13)

## LOGICAL OPERATORS OR BITWISE OPERATORS

In Python, logical operators are used to determine if a conditional statement is true or false. Python's logical operators are AND, OR, and NOT. The following condition is applied to logical operators. For the AND operator, it returns TRUE if both operands (right and left) are true. The OR operator returns TRUE if either of the operands (right or left) is true. If the operand is false, the NOT operator returns TRUE.

Example: In this case, we receive true or false based on the values of a and b.

```
a = True
b = False
print(('a and b is',a and b))
print(('a or b is',a or b))
print(('not a is',not a))
```

Output :

('a and b is', False)

('a or b is', True)

('not a is', False)

## MEMBERSHIP OPERATORS

This operators check for sequence membership, such as lists, strings, or tuples. Python has two membership operators that are utilized. (in, not in). It returns a result depending on the variable in the supplied sequence or text.

For example, using the in and not in operators, we may determine if the values x=4 and y=8 are accessible in the list.

```
x = 4
y = 8
list = [1, 2, 3, 4, 5 ];
if ( x in list ):
    print("Line 1 - x is available in the given list")
else:
    print("Line 1 - x is not available in the given list")
if ( y not in list ):
    print("Line 2 - y is not available in the given list")
else:
    print("Line 2 - y is available in the given list")
```

Outlook:

Line 1 - x is available in the given list

Line 2 - y is not available in the given list

- Declare the value for x and y

167

- Declare the value of list
- Use the "in" operator in code with if statement to check the value of x existing in the list and print the result accordingly
- Use the "not in" operator in code with if statement to check the value of y exist in the list and print the result accordingly
- Run the code- When the code run it gives the desired output

## IDENTITY OPERATORS

Identity Operators are used in Python to compare the memory locations of two objects. Python's two identity operators are (is, is not).

- Operator is: It returns true if two variables point the same object and false otherwise
- Operator is not: It returns false if two variables point the same object and true otherwise

The operands that follow are listed in decreasing order of precedence. Left to right evaluation of operators in the same box

| Operators (Decreasing order of precedence) | Meaning |
|---|---|
| ** | Exponent |
| *, /, //, % | Multiplication, Division, Floor division, Modulus |
| +, − | Addition, Subtraction |
| <= <>>= | Comparison operators |
| = %= /= //= -= += *= **= | Assignment Operators |
| is is not | Identity operators |
| in not in | Membership operators |
| not or and | Logical operators |

Example:
```
x = 20
y = 20
if ( x is y ):
    print("x & y  SAME identity")
y=30
if ( x is not y ):
    print("x & y have DIFFERENT identity")
```

Output :
x & y SAME identity

168

x & y have DIFFERENT identity

- Declare the value for variable x and y
- Use the operator "is" in code to check if value of x is same as y
- Next we use the operator "is not" in code if value of x is not same as y
- Run the code- The output of the result is as expected

## OPERATOR PRECEDENCE

Which operators must be evaluated first are determined by the operator precedence. Precedence operators is required to avoid value ambiguity. Multiplication takes precedence over addition, just as it does in the standard multiplication approach. For example, in 3+4*5, the answer is 23, but we may shift the order of priority by using parenthesis (3+4)*5, which yields 35. Python's precedence operators include (unary + -, **, * /%, + -, &) and others.

```
v = 4
w = 5
x = 8
y = 2
z = 0
z = (v+w) * x / y;
print("Value of (v+w) * x/ y is ",  z)
```

Output:
('Value of (v+w) * x/ y is ', 36)
Declare the value of variable v,w…z
Now execute the code and apply the formula.
The code will run and compute the variable with the highest precedence, returning the result.

## CHAPTER TWELVE: UNDERSTAND THE CONTROL FLOW STATEMENTS

In real life, we face circumstances in which we must make decisions and then determine what to do next. Similar circumstances exist in programming where we must make judgments and then execute the following block of code depending on that decisions. In programming languages, decision-making statements determine the direction (Control Flow) of program execution.

## TYPES OF CONTROL FLOW

The following are examples of control flow statements in the Python programming language:

- The if statement
- The if-else statement
- The nested-if statement
- The if-elif-else ladder

**IF STATEMENT**

The simplest basic decision-making statement is the if statement. It is used to determine whether or not a certain statement or block of statements will be performed.
Syntax:
if condition:
  # Statements to execute if
  # condition is true
In this case, the condition will be either true or false after examination. If the statement takes boolean values, if the value is true, the block of statements below it will be executed; otherwise, it will not. Python, as we know, employs indentation to indicate a block. As a result, the block within an if statement will be recognized as demonstrated in the following example:
if condition:
  statement1
statement2
# Here if the condition is true, if block
# will consider only statement1 to be inside
# its block.

# Flowchart of Python if statement

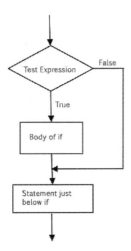

## Example of Python if Statement

```
# python program to illustrate If statement

i = 10

if (i > 15):
    print("10 is less than 15")
print("I am Not in if")
```

Because the condition in the if expression is false. As a result, the block after the if statement is executed.

Output:
I am Not in if

## IF-ELSE STATEMENT

The if statement alone tells us that if a condition is true, a block of statements will be executed; if the condition is false, the block of statements will not be executed. However, if we want to do something different if the condition is false, we may use the else statement in conjunction with the if statement to run a block of code when the if condition is false.

Syntax:
if (condition):
    # Executes this block if
    # condition is true
else:
    # Executes this block if
    # condition is false

171

**Flowchart of Python if-else statement**

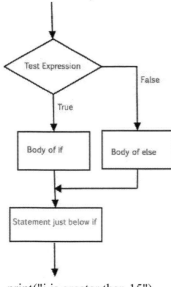

Example of Python if-else statement
When the condition in the if statement is false after invoking the statement that is not in the block (without spaces), the block of code after the else statement is performed.

```
# python program to illustrate If else
statement
#!/usr/bin/python
i = 20
if (i < 15):
 print("i is smaller than 15")
 print("i'm in if Block")
else:
 print("i is greater than 15")
 print("i'm in else Block")
print("i'm not in if and not in else Block")
```

Output:
i is greater than 15
i'm in else Block
i'm not in if and not in else Block

Example of Python if else statement in a list comprehension

```
# Explicit function
def digitSum(n):
 dsum = 0
 for ele in str(n):
  dsum += int(ele)
 return dsum
# Initializing list
List = [367, 111, 562, 945, 6726, 873]
# Using the function on odd elements of the list
newList = [digitSum(i) for i in List if i & 1]
# Displaying new list
print(newList)
```

Output
[16, 3, 18, 18]

## NESTED-IF STATEMENT

An if statement that is the target of another if statement is referred to as a nested if. Nested if statements are if statements that are included within another if statement. Yes, we may stack if statements within if statements in Python. In other words, we may nest an if statement within another if statement.

Syntax:

```
if (condition1):
    # Executes when condition1 is true
    if (condition2):
        # Executes when condition2 is true
    # if Block is end here
# if Block is end here
```

## Flowchart of Python Nested if Statement

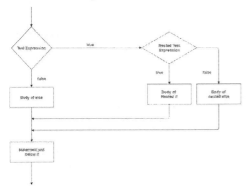

### Example of Python Nested if statement

```
# python program to illustrate nested If statement
#!/usr/bin/python
i = 10
if (i == 10):

    # First if statement
    if (i < 15):
        print("i is smaller than 15")

    # Nested - if statement
    # Will only be executed if statement above
    # it is true
    if (i < 12):
        print("i is smaller than 12 too")
    else:
        print("i is greater than 15")
```

Output:
i is smaller than 15
i is smaller than 12 too

## IF-ELIF-ELSE LADDER

A user can select from a number of alternatives here. The if statements are performed in the order listed. When one of the if conditions is met, the statement associated with that if is performed, and the rest of the ladder is skipped. If none of the requirements are met, the last else expression is performed.

Syntax:

```
if (condition):
    statement
```

173

elif (condition):
    statement

.

.

else:
    statement

**Flowchart of Python if-elif-else ladder**

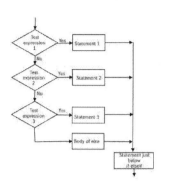

**Example of Python if-elif-else ladder**

Output:
i is 20

**SHORT HAND IF STATEMENT**

When there is only one statement to be performed

```
# Python program to illustrate if-elif-else ladder
#!/usr/bin/python

i = 20
if (i == 10):
    print("i is 10")
elif (i == 15):
    print("i is 15")
elif (i == 20):
    print("i is 20")
else:
    print("i is not present")
```

within an if block, abbreviated if can be utilized. The if statement and the statement can be placed on the same line.
Syntax:
if condition: statement
Example of Python if shorthand

```
# Python program to illustrate short hand if
i = 10
if i < 15: print("i is less than 15")
```

Output:
i is less than 1

## SHORT HAND IF-ELSE STATEMENT

This may be used to create if-else statements on a single line when just one statement is required in both the if and else blocks.
Syntax:
statement_when_True if condition else statement_when_False

Example of Python if else shorthand

```python
# Python program to illustrate short hand if-else
i = 10
print(True) if i < 15 else print(False)
```

Output:
True

# CHAPTER THIRTEEN: UNDERSTAND THE LOOPS IN PYTHON

There is no C-style for loop in Python, such as for (i=0; I n; i++). There has a "for" loop, which is comparable to other languages' loops. Let's look at how to utilize a loop to do consecutive traversals.

## FOR LOOPS IN PYTHON

The Python For loop is used for sequential traversal, that is, iterating over an iterable such as a String, Tuple, List, Set, or Dictionary.
For loops in Python only support collection-based iteration.
For Loops Syntax
for var in iterable:
 # statements

### Flowchart of for loop

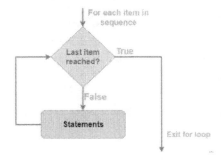

The iterable in this case is a collection of objects such as lists and tuples. The for loops' indented statements are performed once for each item in an iterable. Each time the loop is executed, the variable var is set to the value of the iterable's next item.

## EXAMPLES OF PYTHON FOR LOOP

Python For Loop with List
This code used a for loop to cycle through a list of strings, outputting each item on a new line. The loop adds each item to the variable I and repeats until the entire list has been handled.

```
# Python program to illustrate
# Iterating over a list
l = ["micks", "for", "micks"]
for i in l:
 print(i)
```

Output :
micks
for
micks

## PYTHON FOR LOOP IN PYTHON DICTIONARY

A for loop is used in this code to cycle through a dictionary and output each key-value pair on a new line. The loop assigns each key to the variable i and prints the key and its matching value using string formatting.

```
# Iterating over dictionary
print("Dictionary Iteration")
d = dict()
d['xyz'] = 123
d['abc'] = 345
for i in d:
 print("% s % d" % (i, d[i]))
```

Output:

```
Dictionary Iteration
xyz  123
abc  345
```

## PYTHON FOR LOOP IN PYTHON STRING

A for loop is used in this code to iterate through a string and output each character on a new line. The loop assigns each character to the variable i and repeats until the entire string has been handled.

```
# Iterating over a String
print("String Iteration")
s = "micks"
for i in s:
 print(i)
```

Output:

```
String Iteration
M
I
c
k
s
```

## PYTHON FOR LOOP WITH A STEP SIZE

This code used a for loop and the range() function to create a sequence of numbers ranging from 0 to (but not including) 10, with a step size of 2. The print() method is used by the loop to print the value of each number in the series. The numbers 0, 2, 4, 6, and 8 will be shown in the output.

```
for i in range(0, 10, 2):
```

```
print(i)
```
Output :
0
2
4
6
8

## PYTHON FOR LOOP INSIDE A FOR LOOP

This code iterates over two ranges of numbers (1 to 3 inclusive) and outputs the value of i and j for each combination of the two loops using stacked for loops. For each value of i in the outer loop, the inner loop is run. As each value of i is coupled with each value of j, the result of this code will print the numbers 1 to 3 three times.

```
for i in range(1, 4):
 for j in range(1, 4):
  print(i, j)
```
Output :
1 1
1 2
1 3
2 1
2 2
2 3
3 1
3 2
3 3

## PYTHON FOR LOOP WITH ZIP()

The zip() method is used in this code to iterate over two lists (fruits and colors) in simultaneously. In each iteration, the for loop assigns the matching entries of both lists to the variables fruit and color. The print() method is used within the loop to show the message "is" between the fruit and color values. Each fruit from the list of fruits will be displayed, along with its appropriate color from the colors list.

```
fruits = ["apple", "banana", "cherry"]
colors = ["red", "yellow", "green"]
for fruit, color in zip(fruits, colors):
 print(fruit, "is", color)
```

Output :
apple is red
banana is yellow
cherry is green

## PYTHON FOR LOOP WITH TUPLE

Using a for loop and tuple unpacking, this code iterates over a tuple of tuples. The values from the inner tuple are set to variables a and b in each iteration, and then written to the console using the print() method. Each pair of values from the inner tuples will be displayed in the output.

```
t = ((1, 2), (3, 4), (5, 6))
for a, b in t:
    print(a, b)
```
Output :
1 2
3 4
5 6

## LOOP CONTROL STATEMENTS

The execution of loop control statements differs from the regular order. All automated objects produced in that scope are deleted when execution exits that scope. Python provides the control statements listed below.

Python for Loop with Continue Statement

The continue statement in Python returns control to the beginning of the loop.

```
# Prints all letters except 'e' and 's'
for letter in 'micksformicks':
 if letter == 'e' or letter == 's':
  continue
 print('Current Letter :', letter)
```
Output:
Current Letter : m
Current Letter : k
Current Letter : f
Current Letter : o
Current Letter : r
Current Letter : m
Current Letter : k

# PYTHON FOR LOOP WITH BREAK STATEMENT

The Python break statement removes control from the loop.

```
for letter in 'micksformicks':
# break the loop as soon it sees 'e'
# or 's'
if letter == 'e' or letter == 's':
  break
print('Current Letter :', letter)
```

Output:

Current Letter : e

# PYTHON FOR LOOP WITH PASS STATEMENT

The pass statement is used to create empty loops. Pass is also used for control statements, functions, and classes that are empty.

```
# An empty loop
for letter in 'micksformicks':
pass
print('Last Letter :', letter)
```

Output:

Last Letter : s

Python for loop with range function

The Python range() method is used to construct a numeric series. Depending on how many arguments the user passes to the function, the user may choose where the sequence of numbers begins and ends, as well as how much difference there is between one number and the next.range() accepts three parameters in total.

- Start: integer starting from which the sequence of integers is to be returned
- Stop: integer before which the sequence of integers is to be returned.
- The range of integers ends at a stop – 1.
- Step: integer value which determines the increment between each integer in the sequence.

```
# Python Program to
# show range() basics
# printing a number
for i in range(10):
 print(i, end=" ")
```

```
# performing sum of first 10 numbers
sum = 0
for i in range(1, 10):
 sum = sum + i
print("\nSum of first 10 numbers :", sum)
```
Output:
0 1 2 3 4 5 6 7 8 9
Sum of first 10 numbers : 45

## ELSE WITH FOR LOOP IN PYTHON

Python also supports the else condition in loops. When the loop is not stopped by a break statement, the else block immediately after for/while is run.
```
# Python program to demonstrate
# for-else loop
for i in range(1, 4):
 print(i)
else: # Executed because no break in for
 print("No Break\n")
```
Output:
1
2
3
No Break

## WHILE LOOP

The Python While Loop is used to run a set of statements continuously until a condition is met. When the condition is met, the line immediately after the loop in the program is performed.
Syntax:
```
while expression:
    statement(s)
```

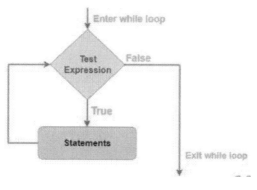

**Flowchart of While Loop :**

Within the realm of programming, the while loop falls under the realm of indefinite iteration.

182

This classification implies that the precise number of times the loop will execute is not explicitly predetermined.

In Python, a block of code is composed of statements that are indented by the same number of character spaces after a programming construct. This indentation serves as a means of grouping statements together. When a while loop is executed, an expression (expr) is initially evaluated within a Boolean context. If the expression evaluates to true, the loop's body is executed. Subsequently, the expression is reevaluated, and if it remains true, the body is executed once again. This process continues until the expression eventually becomes false, at which point the loop terminates.

Example 1: Python While Loop

```
# Python program to illustrate
# while loop
count = 0
while (count < 3):
    count = count + 1
    print("Hello mick")
```

Output

Hello mick
Hello mick
Hello mick

In the preceding example, the while condition will be True as long as the counter variable (count) is less than 3.

Example 2: Python while loop with list

```
# checks if list still
# contains any element
a = [1, 2, 3, 4]
while a:
    print(a.pop())
```

Output

4
3
2
1

In the preceding example, we ran a while loop over a list that would continue until there is an element in the list.

Example 3: Single statement while block

If the while block consists of a single statement, we may define the entire loop in a single line, much like the if block. If there are numerous statements in the loop body block, they can be separated by semicolons (;).

```
# Python program to illustrate
```

```
# Single statement while block
count = 0
while (count <5): count += 1; print("Hello mick")
```
Output
Hello mick
Hello mick
Hello mick
Hello mick
Hello mick

Example 4: Loop Control Statements

Loop control statements alter the execution sequence. All automated objects produced in that scope are deleted when execution exits that scope. Python provides the control statements listed below.

## CONTINUE STATEMENT

Python's Continue Statement restores control to the loop's beginning.
Python while loop with continue statement as an example

```
# Prints all letters except 'e' and 's'
i = 0
a = 'micksformicks'

while i < len(a):
 if a[i] == 'e' or a[i] == 's':
  i += 1
  continue
 print('Current Letter :', a[i])
 i += 1
```
Output
Current Letter : m
Current Letter : k
Current Letter : f
Current Letter : o
Current Letter : r
Current Letter : m
Current Letter : k

## BREAK STATEMENT

The Python Break Statement removes control from the loop. Python while loop with a break statement as an example
# break the loop as soon it sees 'e'

```
# or 's'
i = 0
a = 'micksformicks'

while i < len(a):
 if a[i] == 'e' or a[i] == 's':
  i += 1
  break
 print('Current Letter :', a[i])
 i += 1
Output
Current Letter : m
```

## PASS STATEMENT

Python's pass statement is used to create empty loops. Pass is also used for control statements, functions, and classes that are empty.
Python while loop with a pass statement as an example

```
# An empty loop
a = 'micksformicks'
i = 0
while i < len(a):
 i += 1
 pass
print('Value of i :', i)
Output
Value of i : 13
```

## WHILE LOOP WITH ELSE

As previously stated, a while loop performs the block till a condition is met. When the condition is false, the statement that follows the loop is performed. When your while condition fails, the else clause is performed. If you exit the loop or throw an error, the code will not be performed.
Please keeps in mind that the else block immediately after for/while is only run when the loop is NOT ended by a break statement.

```
# Python program to demonstrate
# while-else loop
i = 0
while i < 4:
 i += 1
 print(i)
```

```
else: # Executed because no break in for
 print("No Break\n")
i = 0
while i < 4:
 i += 1
 print(i)
 break
else: # Not executed as there is a break
 print("No Break")
```
Output
1
2
3
4
No Break
1

```
Enter a number (-1 to quit): 6
Enter a number (-1 to quit): 7
Enter a number (-1 to quit): 8
Enter a number (-1 to quit): 9
Enter a number (-1 to quit): 10
Enter a number (-1 to quit): -1
```

## SENTINEL
## CONTROLLED STATEMENT

We doesn't need a counter variable in this since we don't know how many times the loop will run. The user specifies how many times the loop should be executed. We use a sentinel value for this. A sentinel value is a value that is used to stop a loop once a user enters it; the sentinel value is typically -1.

Python while loop with user input as an example

```
a = int(input('Enter a number (-1 to quit): '))
while a != -1:
 a = int(input('Enter a number (-1 to quit): '))
```
Output:


**Explanation:**

- First, it asks the user to input a number. if the user enters -1 then the loop will not execute
- User enter 6 and the body of the loop executes and again ask for input
- Here user can input many times until he enters -1 to stop the loop
- User can decide how many times he wants to enter input

Example: While loop on Boolean values:

Boolean values are commonly used in while loops to create an infinite loop that can only be exited based on some condition within the loop. As an example:

```
# Initialize a counter
count = 0
# Loop infinitely
while True:
 # Increment the counter
 count += 1
 print(f"Count is {count}")
 # Check if the counter has reached a certain value
 if count == 10:
  # If so, exit the loop
  break
# This will be executed after the loop exits
print("The loop has ended.")
```

Output
Count is 1
Count is 2
Count is 3
Count is 4
Count is 5
Count is 6
Count is 7
Count is 8
Count is 9
Count is 10
The loop has ended.

## CHAPTER FOURTEEN: ADVANTAGES AND APPLICATIONS OF THE PYTHON PROGRAMMING LANGUAGE

Python is a dynamic programming language that is high-level, interpreted, and focused on code readability. When compared to Java and C, it has smaller programs. Guido Van Rossum, a developer, started it in 1991. Python is one of the world's most popular and fastest-growing programming languages.

Python is a sophisticated, adaptable, and user-friendly programming language. Furthermore, the Python community is quite active. It is widely utilized in many companies since it supports a variety of programming paradigms. It also manages memory automatically.

### ADVANTAGES

- Presence of third-party modules
- Extensive support libraries(NumPy for numerical calculations, Pandas for data analytics, etc.)
- Open source and large active community base
- Versatile, Easy to read, learn and write
- User-friendly data structures
- High-level language
- Dynamically typed language(No need to mention data type based on the value assigned, it takes data type)
- Object-Oriented and Procedural Programming language
- Portable and Interactive
- Ideal for prototypes – provide more functionality with less coding
- Highly Efficient(Python's clean object-oriented design provides enhanced process control, and the language is equipped with excellent text processing and integration capabilities, as well as its unit testing framework, which makes it more efficient.) Internet of Things(IoT) Opportunities
- Interpreted Language
- Portable across Operating systems

## DISADVANTAGES

### Performance

Python is an interpreted language, therefore it may be slower than compiled languages such as C or Java. This can be a problem for jobs that need a lot of performance.

### Global Interpreter Lock

The Global Interpreter Lock (GIL) is a Python mechanism that prohibits several threads from executing Python code at the same time. Some applications' parallelism and concurrency may be limited as a result.

### Memory consumption

Python has a high memory consumption, especially when dealing with huge datasets or performing sophisticated algorithms.

### Dynamically typed

Python is a dynamically typed language, which implies that variable types can change during execution. This can make detecting problems more complex and lead to bugs.

### Packaging and versioning

Python has a huge number of packages and libraries, which can cause versioning problems and package conflicts.

### Lack of strictness

Python's adaptability may be a double-edged sword at times. While it might be useful for quick development and experimentation, it can also result in difficult-to-read and maintain code.

### Steep learning curve

While Python is typically regarded as a very simple language to learn, it may nonetheless have a high learning curve for newcomers, particularly those with no prior programming expertise.

## APPLICATIONS

- GUI-based desktop applications
- Graphic design, image processing applications, Games, and Scientific/ computational Applications
- Web frameworks and applications
- Enterprise and Business applications
- Operating Systems
- Education
- Database Access
- Language Development
- Prototyping

- Software Development
- Data Science and Machine Learning
- Scripting

## ORGANIZATIONS USING PYTHON

- Google(Components of Google spider and Search Engine)
- Yahoo(Maps)
- YouTube
- Mozilla
- Dropbox
- Microsoft
- Cisco
- Spotify
- Quora
- Facebook

# CHAPTER FIFTEEN: SIMPLE CALCULATOR PROGRAM USING PYTHON

In this chapter, we will create a simple calculator that can do fundamental arithmetic operations like as addition, subtraction, multiplication, and division.

Example 1) GUI of a Calculator Which will help to add, subtract , Multiply and divide

```python
# pip install tkinter
import tkinter as tk
import tkinter.messagebox
from tkinter.constants import SUNKEN
window = tk.Tk()
window.title('Calculator-micksFormicks')
frame = tk.Frame(master=window, bg="skyblue", padx=10)
frame.pack()
entry = tk.Entry(master=frame, relief=SUNKEN, borderwidth=3,
width=30)
entry.grid(row=0, column=0, columnspan=3, ipady=2, pady=2)
def myclick(number):
 entry.insert(tk.END, number)
def equal():
 try:
  y = str(eval(entry.get()))
  entry.delete(0, tk.END)
  entry.insert(0, y)
 except:
  tkinter.messagebox.showinfo("Error", "Syntax Error")
def clear():
 entry.delete(0, tk.END)
button_1 = tk.Button(master=frame, text='1', padx=15,
    pady=5, width=3, command=lambda: myclick(1))
button_1.grid(row=1, column=0, pady=2)
button_2 = tk.Button(master=frame, text='2', padx=15,
    pady=5, width=3, command=lambda: myclick(2))
button_2.grid(row=1, column=1, pady=2)
button_3 = tk.Button(master=frame, text='3', padx=15,
    pady=5, width=3, command=lambda: myclick(3))
button_3.grid(row=1, column=2, pady=2)
button_4 = tk.Button(master=frame, text='4', padx=15,
    pady=5, width=3, command=lambda: myclick(4))
```

```python
button_4.grid(row=2, column=0, pady=2)
button_5 = tk.Button(master=frame, text='5', padx=15,
    pady=5, width=3, command=lambda: myclick(5))
button_5.grid(row=2, column=1, pady=2)
button_6 = tk.Button(master=frame, text='6', padx=15,
    pady=5, width=3, command=lambda: myclick(6))
button_6.grid(row=2, column=2, pady=2)
button_7 = tk.Button(master=frame, text='7', padx=15,
    pady=5, width=3, command=lambda: myclick(7))
button_7.grid(row=3, column=0, pady=2)
button_8 = tk.Button(master=frame, text='8', padx=15,
    pady=5, width=3, command=lambda: myclick(8))
button_8.grid(row=3, column=1, pady=2)
button_9 = tk.Button(master=frame, text='9', padx=15,
    pady=5, width=3, command=lambda: myclick(9))
button_9.grid(row=3, column=2, pady=2)
button_0 = tk.Button(master=frame, text='0', padx=15,
    pady=5, width=3, command=lambda: myclick(0))
button_0.grid(row=4, column=1, pady=2)
button_add = tk.Button(master=frame, text="+", padx=15,
    pady=5, width=3, command=lambda: myclick('+'))
button_add.grid(row=5, column=0, pady=2)
button_subtract = tk.Button(
 master=frame, text="-", padx=15, pady=5, width=3, command=lambda:
myclick('-'))
button_subtract.grid(row=5, column=1, pady=2)
button_multiply = tk.Button(
 master=frame, text="*", padx=15, pady=5, width=3, command=lambda:
myclick('*'))
button_multiply.grid(row=5, column=2, pady=2)
button_div = tk.Button(master=frame, text="/", padx=15,
    pady=5, width=3, command=lambda: myclick('/'))
button_div.grid(row=6, column=0, pady=2)
button_clear = tk.Button(master=frame, text="clear",
    padx=15, pady=5, width=12, command=clear)
button_clear.grid(row=6, column=1, columnspan=2, pady=2)
button_equal = tk.Button(master=frame, text="=", padx=15,
    pady=5, width=9, command=equal)
button_equal.grid(row=7, column=0, columnspan=3, pady=2)
```

window.mainloop()
Output:

**Time complexity**

The amount of processes performed in the computation determines the temporal complexity of this calculator. Basic operations like addition, subtraction, multiplication, and division have a temporal complexity of O(1). The time complexity of more sophisticated calculations requiring several operations will be greater.

**Space complexity**

This calculator's space complexity is O(1). This is because the calculator just has to keep the user input and the calculation output, which can be done with a little amount of memory.

**Example 2:** Create a basic calculator that can do fundamental arithmetic operations like as addition, subtraction, multiplication, and division based on user input. Approach:

- User chooses the desired operation. Options 1, 2, 3, and 4 are valid.
- Two numbers are taken and an if...elif...else branching is used to execute a particular section.
- Using functions add(), subtract(), multiply() and divide() evaluate respective operations.

*Please select operation:*

1. Add
2. Subtract
3. Multiply
4. Divide

Select operations form 1, 2, 3, 4 : 1
Enter first number : 20
Enter second number : 13
20 + 13 = 33
# Python program for simple calculator
# Function to add two numbers
def add(num1, num2):
    return num1 + num2

195

```python
# Function to subtract two numbers
def subtract(num1, num2):
    return num1 - num2
# Function to multiply two numbers
def multiply(num1, num2):
    return num1 * num2
# Function to divide two numbers
def divide(num1, num2):
    return num1 / num2
print("Please select operation -\n" \
    "1. Add\n" \
    "2. Subtract\n" \
    "3. Multiply\n" \
    "4. Divide\n")
# Take input from the user
select = int(input("Select operations form 1, 2, 3, 4 :"))
number_1 = int(input("Enter first number: "))
number_2 = int(input("Enter second number: "))
if select == 1:
    print(number_1, "+", number_2, "=",
                add(number_1, number_2))
elif select == 2:
    print(number_1, "-", number_2, "=",
                subtract(number_1, number_2))

elif select == 3:
    print(number_1, "*", number_2, "=",
                multiply(number_1, number_2))
elif select == 4:
    print(number_1, "/", number_2, "=",
divide(number_1, number_2))
else:
    print("Invalid input")
```
Output:
Please select operation -
Add
Subtract
Multiply
Divide
Select operations form 1, 2, 3, 4 : 1
Enter first number : 15

Enter second number : 14

15 + 14 = 29

**Time Complexity: O(1)**

The time complexity of this program is O(1) as it has a constant time to execute the given statements regardless of the input.

Space Complexity: O(1)

The program uses a constant amount of space regardless of the input, so the space complexity is O(1).

# Chapter Sixteen: BIRTHDAY REMINDER APPLICATION USING PYTHON

This software may remind you of your birthdays and alert you of your friends' birthdays. This program utilizes Python and Ubuntu notifications to tell users when the system boots up.

```python
# Python program For
# Birthday Reminder Application
# time module is must as reminder
# is set with the help of dates
import time
# os module is used to notify user
# using default "Ubuntu" notification bar
import os
# Birthday file is the one in which the actual birthdays
# and dates are present. This file can be
# manually edited or can be automated.
# For simplicity, we will edit it manually.
# Birthdays should be written in this file in
# the format: "MonthDay Name Surname" (Without Quotes)
birthdayFile = '/path/to/birthday/file'
def checkTodaysBirthdays():
    fileName = open(birthdayFile, 'r')
    today = time.strftime('%m%d')
    flag = 0
    for line in fileName:
        if today in line:
            line = line.split(' ')
            flag =1
            # line[1] contains Name and line[2] contains Surname
            os.system('notify-send "Birthdays Today: ' + line[1]
            + ' ' + line[2] + '"')
    if flag == 0:
        os.system('notify-send "No Birthdays Today!"')
if __name__ == '__main__':
    checkTodaysBirthdays()
```

## ADDING THE SCRIPT TO STARTUP

It is now time to add this Python script to startup after creating the aforementioned code. This is possible on Ubuntu by doing the following:

- Firstly, we have to create an executable file for our reminder.py script
- This can be done by typing the following command in the terminal

sudo chmod +x reminder.py, where reminder.py is our script file name

- Now we have to transfer this file to the path where Linux searches for its default files:

Type this command in terminal:
sudo cp /path/to/our/reminder.py /usr/bin
. This will add our executable script to /usr/bin.

- In global search, search for Startup Applications
- Click on Add and Give a desired Name for your process
- Type in the command. For example, our file name is reminder.py then type reminder.py in the command field and Select Add

Note: When you start your system, the script runs automatically (once added to startup). Also, if you have more than two birthdays on the same day, the notice will include both of them.
How the birthday file should look like and Output after running the script.

# CONCLUSION

Python is now the most extensively used multi-purpose, high-level programming language, with Object-Oriented and Procedural programming paradigms. Python applications are often smaller than those written in other programming languages such as Java. Programmers must type relatively little, and the language's indentation requirement ensures that their code is always understandable.

Basics, Input/Output, Data Types, Variables, Operators, Control Flow, Functions, Object Oriented Concepts, Exception Handling, Python Collections, Django Framework, Data Analysis, Numpy, Pandas, Machine Learning with Python, Python GUI, Modules in Python, Working with Database, Misc, Applications and Projects, Multiple Choice Questions Python is a high-level, general-purpose, and very popular programming language. Python programming language (latest Python 3) is being used in web development, Machine Learning applications, along with all cutting-edge technology in Software Industry.

Python language is being used by almost all tech-giant companies like – Google, Amazon, Facebook, Instagram, Dropbox, Uber... etc.

*Python's greatest strength is its vast set of standard libraries, which may be used for the following:*

- Machine Learning
- GUI Applications (like Kivy, Tkinter, PyQt etc. )
- Web frameworks like Django (used by YouTube, Instagram, Dropbox)
- Image processing (like OpenCV, Pillow)
- Web scraping (like Scrapy, BeautifulSoup, Selenium)
- Test frameworks
- Multimedia
- Scientific computing

Text processing and many more.

# BONUS

# EMPOWERING YOUR LIFE

## HARNESSING THE POWER OF CHAT GPT AND PYTHON TO CREATE YOUR PERSONAL ASSISTANT

Download the PDF to learn more about how Python and AI interact dynamically to create your personal assistant. This in-depth manual explores the effective interplay between Python, a flexible programming language, and AI creation. Learn how Python's large library of tools, including TensorFlow, PyTorch, and NLTK, supports text processing, machine learning, and NLU. Learn how to create writing that is coherent and contextually appropriate using Chat GPT, a potent language model created by OpenAI. This book gives you the tools to create a customized and intelligent assistant, from controlling conversation flow to interacting with numerous platforms. Start your journey toward maximizing Python and AI's combined potential by downloading the PDF right away.

## Thank You for Reading!

I hope you found my book on Python both informative and enjoyable. Your support means the world to me, and I'm grateful for the opportunity to share my knowledge with you.

If you found this book helpful, please consider **leaving a review on Amazon**. Your feedback not only helps other readers make informed decisions, but it also enables me to keep improving the content and provide even better resources for the Python community.

Leaving a review is quick and easy:

Visit the book's Amazon page here.
Scroll down to the "Customer reviews" section and click "Write a customer review."
Rate the book on a scale of 1 to 5 stars and provide your honest feedback on what you liked, what you learned, and any suggestions for improvement.
Every review, no matter how brief, truly makes a difference. Thank you for taking the time to share your thoughts and for supporting my work!

Happy coding, and I hope to hear from you soon!